A Peircean Reduction Thesis

PHILOSOPHICAL
INQUIRIES

A Peircean Reduction Thesis
The Foundations of Topological Logic

Robert W. Burch

TEXAS TECH UNIVERSITY PRESS

Philosophical Inquiries

Number 1

Series Editor
Kenneth Laine Ketner

Library of Congress Catalogining-in-Publication Data
Burch, Robert W.
   Peirce's reduction thesis : the foundations of topological logic /
Robert W. Burch
      p.   cm. — (Philosophical inquiries ; no. 1)
   Includes bibliographical references.
   ISBN 0-89672-247-3
   1. Algebraic logic. I. Title. II. Series.
QA10.B86 1991
511.3—dc20   90-26949
                                                         CIP

Texas Tech University Press
Lubbock, Texas 79409-1037, USA

DEDICATION

This work is dedicated to Carolyn Eisele and Kenneth Ketner

Carolyn Eisele's whole career as a Peirce scholar has been devoted to showing, repeatedly and irrefutably, that one cannot understand Peirce exactly without understanding his mathematics. This work would not have been possible without her urging. It was inspired by her kindness and her strength of character. May this work be an expression to her of my deepest admiration.

Kenneth Ketner showed me for the first time the real Peirce. He indicated to me the connection between Peirce's logic and Listing's topology and aided me in every way in my investigations of Peirce's existential graphs. He provided all the textual signposts on the path to Peirce's reduction thesis, and pushed me along every step of the way. He saw years ago what lay at the end of this path. May this work be an expression to him of my deepest gratitude.

ACKNOWLEDGMENTS

I am indebted to many persons who in their several ways helped me with this work. I would like to thank Hilary Putnam, Hans G. Herzberger, and most especially Thomas McLaughlin for their extraordinary patience in reading earlier versions of this work and for their penetrating comments upon these versions. The comments saved me from several serious blunders and helped me to press toward making the formalism representative of an intensionalist position with regard to relations without, however, resorting to psychological concepts that would go beyond what is standardly acceptable in contemporary logic. (My thanks should not be taken to imply that any of these reviewers agrees with any of the theses of the work or even approves of the work as a whole. And, of course, all blunders that may remain in the work are entirely my own responsibility.) Thanks are also in order to Richard Ketchersid, whose uncanny mathematical radar spotted problems from far off as well as close up; to Christopher Menzel, whose good cheer and technical suggestions were extremely useful; and to H. S. Thayer, whose shrewd philosophical advice helped immeasurably. Also, I have insufficient words to thank my wife Maudie, without whose gentle encouragements the task of composition might not have been so much fun.

THE ANTECEDENTS AND AIMS OF THIS WORK

Charles S. Peirce repeatedly maintained that relations of adicity higher than three could be reduced to relations of adicity three or less, while relations of the first three adicities could not in general be reduced.[1] This claim has seemed to many philosophers to be bizarre in light of various twentieth-century results in logic that show that all relations can be reduced to dyadic ones. There is, for example, the well known reduction to dyadic relations of Quine (1966a). And there is the theorem of Löwenheim, which as a matter of ironic fact Löwenheim proved in terms of an algebraic logic quite similar to Peirce's and derived historically from Peirce's own algebraic logic through the volumes of Schröder.[2] Moreover, although Peirce repeatedly stated that he had proved the claim before 1870, and although Peirce argued for the reduction thesis at some length in his 1870 paper, "Description of a Notation for the Logic of Relatives,"[3] doubt has existed over whether Peirce really did prove the claim.

From the fact that in *some or other* sense of "reduction" all relations can be reduced to dyadic ones, it does not, of course, follow that *Peirce's* claim is wrong or that *his* reduction thesis cannot be proved. For Peirce's understanding of "reduction" might be different from any sense of "reduction" in which wholesale reduction of all relations to the dyadic is possible. Only within the last seven or eight years has progress been made toward a partial vindication of Peirce and an understanding of his own sense of "reduction." Hans G. Herzberger proposed a "bonding algebra" as providing the basis of Peirce's thesis and partially substantiated Peirce by proving a certain version of the thesis correct for domains of sufficiently large cardinality.[4] Kenneth L. Ketner proposed Peirce's existential graphs as basic to understanding Peirce's sense of "reduction" and partially substantiated Peirce by appealing to a notion of "valency analysis" (Ketner, 1986b). By extending both the algebraic ideas of Herzberger and the graph-theoretical ideas of Ketner, this work proposes to develop an algebraic formalism in which a reduction thesis similar to and perhaps identical to the reduction thesis Peirce had in mind can be proved for the general case. This work also proposes to show that the reduction thesis it proves is consistent with the result of Löwenheim and the result of Quine, despite the fact that these results may appear to conflict with it.

This work might best be regarded as a speculative venture toward understanding Peirce's thought. It is not a work of Peirce scholarship in the standard sense: no elaborate references to Peircean texts will be given, and no argument will be mounted that the formalism herein presented duplicates Peirce's own actual formalisms. Delicately sceptical Peirce scholars may feel free to regard this work as an original creation of my own that is inspired by Peirce's logic and especially by Peirce's existential graphs. I am, however, confident that a close study of Peirce's logical writings will indeed tend to confirm that most of this work's details are either accurate or at least approximate representations of Peirce's thinking. Signals to this effect abound: one may note, for example, the role of the COMMA operator, the crucial part played by the teridentity relation, and the use of hypostatic abstraction in the central theorem. Also, the close-to-isomorphic connection established at the end of this work between its main formalism and two systems of graphical representation of that formalism, both of which seem to be very similar to Peirce's existential graphs, should serve to indicate that the substance of Peirce's thought cannot be drastically different from the ideas embodied in the formal structures of this work. It is my hope that the formalism developed in this work may serve Peirce scholars as a template with which Peirce's logical writings may be compared and thereby studied in great detail.

With the exception of Ketner, scholars who have heretofore attempted to understand Peirce's reduction thesis in exact logical terms have tended to have in mind a thesis about relations in the sense of sets of n-tuples. This understanding of relations is an extensionalist understanding. In this work, relations will be understood in *intension*. And, because of this understanding of relations, the work hints that it might be the extensionalist understanding of relations that has prevented scholars so far from achieving more than fragmentary progress toward understanding Peirce's reduction thesis. For Peirce himself did seem to understand relations in an intensional sense. To say this is not to deny that Peirce often analyzed relations in terms of the n-tuples that satisfy these relations. He did so especially in discussing dyadic relations. Nor is it to deny that Peirce meant his reduction thesis to incorporate results about sets of n-tuples. Yet, when Peirce spoke of relations, he never spoke of them simply as *being* sets of n-tuples. Rather, relations for Peirce were something *sui generis*; they were relations *as such*, relations *simpliciter*, relations *period*. Moreover, the *terms* of Peirce's logical algebras were intended to denote or otherwise express such relations *simpliciter*. And it is reasonable to believe that it was relations as such that the primary reduction thesis Peirce had in mind was about. Ketner's studies of Peirce's logical graphs clearly indicate that Peirce intended the graphs as diagrammatic syntax expressive of relations as such (Ketner, 1984).

But what are these relations *simpliciter* that the terms of Peirce's algebras and the pictures of Peirce's graphs express? As far as the formalism of logic goes, the answer to this question will be presented in the sequent formalism of this work. A logical formalism does not of itself, however, answer metaphysical questions. Peirce's full answer to the question as to the nature of relations as such lies in his metaphysics and semeiotic. It is a complex philosophical matter into which this work, owing to the narrowness of its scope, cannot go. One or two remarks, however, are appropriate. Peirce was certainly some sort of realist with regard to relations *simpliciter*, nominalism he rejected with increasing vehemence from at least the mid-1860's. Furthermore, Peirce was a metaphysical foundationalist with regard to relations. In his view, relations as such were fundamental, whereas individual entities were derivative by means of (hypostatic) abstraction from them. At the level of logic, this means that entities, sets, and more generally the whole apparatus of what we now relegate to logical semantics were not primary for Peirce but rather derivative. The apparatus of extensionalism was for Peirce a secondary development dependent upon the logic of relations as such. A full account of what Peirce meant by a relation would have to involve the conception of mind. Because such a factor as mind must be omitted from any account of relations that would have any chance of meeting the criteria of standard logic, the notion of mind is represented in the present work by the notion of an "Interpretation function."

Does the foregoing mean that Peirce was an "intensionalist" in some contemporary sense? I think an affirmative answer would not be completely inappropriate; but to argue in the affirmative prior to a close investigation of Peirce's modal logic would be premature. What is certain was that Peirce was no nominalist, no blind adherent of extensionalist devotion.

May the committed extensionalist therefore turn aside in scorn at this point? I do not think so. For the notion of a relation as such, as the formalism of this work attempts to show, can be explicated consistent with the extensionalism of standard, nominalistic logic.

As Herzberger and Ketner have both recognized, each in his own way, the key to understanding Peirce's reduction thesis is to determine exactly what Peirce meant by "reduction." In other words, the chief task is to determine the definitional resources whereby, in Peirce's view, relations as such may be constructed from other relations as such.

In this connection, Herzberger has come close to an accurate specification: all but perhaps one of Peirce's definitional resources have been given in Herzberger's paper. As Herzberger sees, there was in Peirce's work the vital operation called "relative product," whereby one relation is, as Peirce put it, "applied to" another. There was also what Herzberger calls "bonding." Peirce also had the various permutation operations, which may be reduced to "Major Permutation" and "Minor Permutation," as Herzberger does in following Quine's lead, or left simply as primitively available permutation operations.[5] Finally, there was in Peirce the operation of negation. In many ways, especially in its later theorems, this work should serve to vindicate Herzberger's "bonding algebra" as providing an accurate account of the extensionalist implications of Peirce's theory of relations. For, despite the fact that the operations in the formalism of this work are designed to accord with the operations of Peirce's existential graphs, they can be defined in terms of the operations of "bonding algebra," as, indeed, the operations of "bonding algebra" can be defined in terms of the operations in the formalism of this work.

One Peircean operation that Herzberger seems to include only implicitly is an operation that in this work will be called "arraying." This operation is similar to the operation that is labelled "Zusammenfügung" in the algebraic logic of Bernays (1959). At the level of semantics, arraying appears as the forming of a sort of Cartesian product; in terms of the syntax of quantificational logic, it appears as the formation of conjunctions of well-formed formulae, in which conjunctions every occurrence of a free variable is an occurrence of a distinct variable. The idea will be developed formally in Section 2. One matter that is crucial to appreciate about the definitional resources outlined in this work is that in the process of constructing relations, we are not permitted to apply the operations willy-nilly. The manner of their application is subject to certain detailed restrictions. These restrictions have been motivated by the structure of the existential graphs. The operations of construction and the exact manner in which they may be applied will be presented in the subsequent formal discussions of this work.

NOTES

1. Many examples of the reduction thesis, as asserted by Peirce, are provided in an appendix to Herzberger, 1981.

2. Löwenheim, 1915. The relevant theorem is number 6. This paper is translated in van Heijenoort, 1966, pp. 232-251, as "On Possibilities in the Calculus of Relatives." The Schröder volumes are reprinted as Schröder, 1966. The historical influence of Peirce is discussed in Putnam, 1982.

3. This paper is numbered P52 in Ketner, 1986c. It is published in Kloesel, *et al.*, 1984, pp. 359-429.

4. Herzberger, 1981. The concept of "sufficiently large cardinality" applies to a domain when its cardinality is at least as great as the cardinality of the relation defined on it that is to be reduced.

5. Quine, 1972. See also Quine, 1971. A related work is Quine, 1966b.

CONTENTS

PREFACE   vii

1 Introduction: Peirce's Logical Project   1

2 Peircean Algebraic Logic: the Fundamental Notions   7

3 Semantics for Peircean Algebraic Logic, Part One   27

4 Semantics for Peircean Algebraic Logic, Part Two   39

5 Degeneracy and the Constructibility of Relations   53

6 The Existence of Non-Degenerate Relations   67

7 Teridentity, the COMMA Operator, and
  Derived Elements   71

8 A Representation Theorem for Peircean
  Algebraic Logic   93

9 Hypostatic Abstraction and the Reduction Theorem   105

10 Thirdness and the Consistency of the Reduction Thesis
   of This Work with Other Results in Logic   117

11 Two Systems of Graphical Syntax for Peircean
   Algebraic Logic   123

CONCLUDING REMARKS: On the Consistency and
  Completeness of Peircean Algebraic Logic
  and its Potential Value   137

BIBLIOGRAPHY   141

INDEX   145

Concepts are capable of being compounded only in a way differing but in one doubtful particular from that in which the so-called "substances"— i.e. species—of organic chemistry are compounded . . . . That respect is that the different bonds and pegs of the Spots of Graphs are different, while those of chemical atoms are believed to be all alike . . . . It will be found that the available evidence is decidedly that Concepts can only be combined through definite "pegs."

Charles Sanders Peirce, 1906
From "Prolegomena to an Apology for Pragmaticism"

But let us leave Russell and Whitehead to work out their own salvation. The criticism which I make on [my own] algebra of dyadic relations, with which I am by no means in love, though I think it is a pretty thing, is that the very triadic relations which it does not recognize it does itself employ.

Charles Sanders Peirce, 1904
From a letter to Victoria Lady Welby

1

INTRODUCTION:
PEIRCE'S LOGICAL PROJECT

Before entering into formal considerations, it is useful to begin by taking a very brief look at Peirce's overall project in logic.

From the 1860s through the 1880s, Peirce's work in logic was mainly toward extending Boolean algebra from being a subject concerned exclusively with monadic relations to being a subject competent to handle relations of arbitrarily great (but finite) adicities. Peirce was in fact the creator of the sort of generalized algebraic logic that has become well known in this century through the work of Tarski (1941, 1952), Lyndon (1950), Henkin (1955), Bernays (1959), Halmos (1962), and others. Herzberger's paper demonstrates also the close affiliation between Peirce's algebraic logic and Quine's functor calculus (Quine, 1971, 1972; see also 1966b).

By 1870, Peirce had developed at least a rudimentary concept of the variable (his "marks of reference"), and by 1883 his student 0. H. Mitchell had (no doubt with Peirce's help) worked out the concept of the quantifier.[1] In the mid-1880s, some of Peirce's logical works employed the quantifier-cum-variable formalism in logical systems that, except for notation and philosophical underpinning, are systems of quantificational logic. Yet quantificational logic never gripped Peirce the way it did the philosophical community some twenty-five years later, when Russell-and-Whitehead's *Principia Mathematica* appeared. Although Peirce admired certain aspects of quantificational logic, he still preferred—until well into the 1890s—algebraic logic.

The reason for this preference was straightforward. In Peirce's estimation the purpose of logic—which he identified with semeiotic—was not to develop an efficient calculus to enable conclusions to be drawn quickly and easily from premises. Rather, the proper task of logic was to analyze and display in the most perspicuous way possible the most elementary and fundamental constituents of reasoning. To be sure, quantification theory provided an elegant and efficient calculus for obtaining conclusions from premises; but it did not, in Peirce's view, give an accurate account of reasoning's most basic elements. For this purpose algebraic logic seemed much the better system, for at least two reasons. First, in algebraic logic, what Peirce considered the most fundamental of all modes of conceptual combination, namely "application" or relative product or what Bernays calls the "Peirce'sche Produkt," is handily represented, rather than represented in the clumsy fashion of quantification theory. Second, the terms of algebraic logic may naturally be understood to stand for *relations*, relations as such; and, given Peirce's realism and foundationalism with regard to relations, it follows in his thinking that reasoning is primarily, most elementarily, reasoning *about relations*. Logic should be in touch with this fact. But quantification theory places individuals at the fundamental level, by virtue of its variables and constants. This, in Peirce's view, is a mistake.

Yet even algebraic logic was very far from being completely satisfying to Peirce in regard to the task he considered to be the proper province of logic. For in his estimation, logic should not only indicate the fundamental constituents of reasoning; it should also display them as vividly and as perspicuously as possible. The ideal, therefore, was a system of logical signs that should display the elements of reasoning by actually, insofar as possible, *resembling* them, by being *"icons"* of them.

To the end of creating an "iconic" or "iconoidal" system of logical signs, Peirce explored, with seemingly endless creativity and stamina, one notational device after another. It was in this connection that Peirce was attracted to the topology of J. B. Listing (who not only coined the word *"Topologie"* but also developed the subject far beyond the point at which Euler had left it), the combinatorial and graph-theoretical investigations of J. J. Sylvester (who was Peirce's colleague at Johns Hopkins from 1879 until 1884), and the diagrammatic mathematics and work on the four-color map problem of DeMorgan's student A. B. Kempe.[2] By late 1896, Peirce had elaborated his own topological and graph-theoretical investigations into two systems of "logical graphs," the "entitative graphs" and the "existential graphs." Although the two systems were equal in scope and power, it was the existential graphs that turned out to be the more iconic, as well as the easier to use. Accordingly, it was in the system of existential graphs that Peirce mainly worked after 1897.

In the existential graphs, the syntax of logic was no longer algebraic. Indeed, it was no longer even linear. Rather, graphical syntax is two-dimensional syntax, requiring a surface rather than a line for its inscription. Peirce showed, and it is easily proved by applying a few results of Kuratowski (1930) and Whitney (1932), that this surface is in the general case a torus of genus n. The graphs, as the subsequent developments of this work suggest, were meant as a *topological syntax* for logic. It seems to have been Peirce's intention to use the existential graphs in connection with mathematical results from topology, such as the Census Theorem of Listing (which is a version of what is today called the "Euler-Poincaré Formula"), for the purposes of metalogical analysis. That this program is potentially a fertile one is partly borne out by the present work.

During the course of Peirce's long and fruitful career, he produced not one mathematical-logical system but rather many such systems. The question naturally arises, of course, as to which, if any, of these systems should be taken as definitive of Peirce's claims, especially as regards the reduction thesis. My contention—the argument for which I must reserve for a future work—is that this question presents a less serious difficulty than one might initially suppose.[3] In my opinion, Peirce's logical writings from about 1865 forward indicate that Peirce's various logical systems are differing attempts to formulate, with clarity and iconicity a vision of logic that itself hardly changed at all. Let us call this vision of logic, which in my opinion remained constant despite the changes in its formulation, Peirce's "Unitary Logical Vision"—ULV, for short.

Peirce seems to have reached ULV quite early in the course of his studies, perhaps even as early as his graduate student days at Harvard in chemistry. What seems to have gripped his mind was an analogy he discerned between the physical composition of chemical ions by bonding and the logical composition of concepts by "application." His study of Kant and DeMorgan, and his intense discussions with his brilliant father, the Harvard mathematician Benjamin Peirce, had already persuaded him that concepts could not be confined to the monadic, but must also include relations of adicity higher than 1. As Frege also did, Peirce came to see the adicity of a relation as a characteristic of its capacity to "bond" or "join." Unlike Frege, Peirce thought of this capacity to "join" as a capacity to join with *other relations*, by "application." And he viewed this capacity as so like the capacity of chemical ions to bond, that the adicity of a relation appeared to him as if it were the number of valental positions in an ion. Thus a relation appeared as a kind of conceptual ion.

In the chemistry of the period, the new concepts of "valency" and "ion" were just being formulated. (On this, see Palmer, 1944, 1965.) Ion bonding was thought to occur pairwise, with each bonding of initially separated ions thus resulting in a unified complex ion whose valental number was 2 less than the sum of the valental numbers of the separated ions. The "Valency Formula"

$$V = V_1 + V_2 - 2$$

thus expresses the valency relations thought to correspond to a single bonding. More generally, multiple bondings, k in number, accomplished on n initially separated ions whose valental numbers are V_1, V_2, . . . , V_n, respectively, are described by the general valency formula:

$$V = V_1 + V_2 + \ldots + V_n - 2k.$$

Given Peirce's ULV, the valency formula must apply as well to the joining of concepts by "application" as to the bonding of ions. In the chemical backdrop of Peirce's ULV the germ of the reduction thesis is already present. For a 1-valent ion bonded with a 1-valent ion gives, by the valency formula, a 0-valent ion, because $1 + 1 - 2 = 0$. A 2-valent ion bonded with a 1-valent ion gives a 1-valent ion, because $2 + 1 - 2 = 1$. And a 2-valent ion bonded with a 2-valent ion gives a 2-valent ion, because $2 + 2 - 2 = 2$. Pairwise bonding, therefore, starting only from 1-valent ions and 2-valent ions, can never give anything but 0-valent ions, 1-valent ions, and 2-valent ions. It is impossible to reach 3-valent ions or ions of higher valental number. Moreover, starting strictly from 1-valent ions, pairwise bonding can never lead to anything but 0-valent ions and 1-valent ions. In this chemical sense, therefore, we have an analogue of the negative part of Peirce's reduction thesis. 1-valent ions cannot be built up from 0-valent ions, because 0-valent ions do not bond at all. 2-valent ions cannot be built up from 0-valent ions and 1-valent ions because of the valency formula. And 3-valent ions cannot be built up from 0-valent ions, 1-valent ions, and 2-valent ions because, again, the valency formula prohibits this.

On the positive side, the valency equations

$$3 + 3 - (2 \times 1) = 4,$$

$$3 + 3 + 3 - (2 \times 2) = 5,$$

$$3 + 3 + 3 + 3 - (2 \times 3) = 6,$$

and so forth, show that at least some n-valent ions for all n greater than or equal to 3 may be combinations by pairwise bonding starting with 1-valent ions, 2-valent ions, *and* 3-valent ions. Of course, this fact is very far from being a justification of the claim that *all* n-valent ions for n greater than or equal to 3 *are* such combinations. But there is a hint, at least, that this is so. And given ULV, the same should obtain for the logical combination of concepts by "application."

ULV and its attendant suggestion of a reduction thesis seem to have constantly functioned, in Peirce's mind, as dominant themes. How literally he took the analogy between logic and chemistry I must leave for others to answer. But it seems undoubtable to me that ULV was a *Leitmotiv* for Peirce's logical systems. The question is whether the vision can be brought down to the solid earth of exact mathematical formulation. Peirce claimed that he had shown that it could be. In the sequel, it will be proved that such a general vision as ULV can be made precise.

In particular, the existential graphs contain sufficient structure for explicating ULV and for proving a reduction thesis that seems to be close enough to Peirce's thesis to be at least useful in understanding Peirce's own thinking. To this end, I develop a system of algebraic logic which will hereinafter be called "Peircean Algebraic Logic," or PAL, for short. PAL is an attempt to amalgamate various systems of logic that Peirce developed over his long career. PAL is specifically designed to accord closely with the existential graphs, and indeed to be translatable in a systematic fashion into two systems of graphical syntax, each of which is closely similar to Peirce's existential graphs. Moreover, PAL allows for the proof in it of theorems, such as Listing's Census Theorem (Listing, 1862), that are essentially topological in nature. Additionally, certain features of PAL are designed specifically to correspond with Bernays's algebraic logic, which in my opinion is closely akin to the logic of Peirce. Examples of these features are the use of Bernays's "Zusammenfügung" notation as one allowable notation for arraying, the use of the notation V^n for the universal classes of n-tuples, and the use of the various empty, or null, n-tuples, labelled $0^{(n)}$ by Bernays and labelled in PAL by $()^n$.

In choosing to elaborate PAL instead of choosing to present Peirce's logic by means of a thoroughgoing textual analysis of any or all of the various logical systems that Peirce historically developed, I have of course chosen to avoid confining the formalism of his presentation to any one of the many systems of algebraic logic that Peirce historically elaborated. PAL is best thought of as relating to Peirce's historical elaborations through the existential graphs, which I assume to be one formulation of ULV.

The position I take is that the value of avoiding elaborate discussion of any one or of many of Peirce's historical systems, and presenting PAL instead, is that this procedure may enable textually sophisticated Peirce scholars to see more clearly and precisely than otherwise might be possible common themes that run through all of Peirce's formalisms. A virtue of

PAL is that it provides a single "generic" formalism with which the various Peircean systems can be handily compared, so that they can all the more easily be compared with one another. Another potentially useful feature of PAL is that it may enable scholars to fill out Peirce's extremely compressed reasoning in sufficient detail to make it more comprehensible. As Peirce wrote out his own thoughts, he tended to condense them so severely that they are often hard to follow. Perhaps Peirce was not really disdainful of exact demonstration; rather, perhaps he simply omitted details that seemed to him excessively easy. But what might have seemed obvious or trivial to a logician of Peirce's genius may not always seem so to a scholarly reader of Peirce. PAL may enable scholars to fill in gaps that Peirce hurried over.

Notes

1. For the notion of "marks of reference," see Kloesel, *et al.*, 1984, p. 372.
2. See Murphey, 1961, ch. 9. Listing's published mathematical work is Listing, 1847, 1862.
3. For a partial defense of this contention, see Robert W. Burch, "Peirce on the Application of Relations to Relations," in *Studies in the Logic of Charles S. Peirce,* ed. Nathan Houser, Don D. Roberts, and James Van Evra (Indiana University Press, 1992).
4. For a comparison of the notations of Frege and Peirce, see Hawkins, 1981.

2

PEIRCEAN ALGEBRAIC LOGIC:
THE FUNDAMENTAL NOTIONS

As the formalism of PAL is read, readers will find it to advantage to refer often to the two graphical systems of syntax for PAL that are presented in Section 11 of this work. This procedure will not only help readers to appreciate the motivation for the various technical constructions in PAL; it will also make the meaning of the constructions of PAL easier to assimilate rapidly. One picture, readers will come to realize, is worth a thousand words. A few further remarks to aid in understanding PAL will now be made.

First, in the following account of PAL, corner-quotes are avoided for ease in readability. Philosophers who are sensitive to use-mention distinctions may supply corner-quotes and amended phrasing as they please. Definitions, propositions, and theorems will be labelled with the section number in which they occur and with their item number in that section. Thus, the fourth proposition of Section 3, for example, will be labelled "Proposition 3.4." Corollaries to theorems will be labelled by theorem number and item number. So the second corollary to the third theorem of Section 7, for example, will be labelled "Corollary 7.3.2." Theorems are distinguished from propositions by virtue of their increment in importance.

Second, finite sequences will play an important role in the following discussions. In these discussions, the convention will be adopted of identifying finite sequences of length 1 with the items that are the sole entry in such sequences. Strictly speaking, of course, this identification makes a leap between two types of mathematical entities. Nevertheless, making this leap allows a number of points and constructions to be made in fairly simple language, whereas adhering strictly to the distinction between items and sequences of length 1 of items would lead to cumbersome language. Those who may be sticklers for exact expression may easily substitute more exact phrasing whenever they feel that their sensitivities about types of mathematical objects are aroused.

Third, a concept of "Cartesian Product" is important for the discussions. Philosophers often insist on a rigid distinction between "Cartesian Product," which they conceive to be always a set of ordered *pairs*, and "Concatenation," which need not be a set only of *pairs*. Mathematicians, on the other hand, do not worry overly much about the distinction. In this work, the practice of mathematicians is followed. The word "concatenation" is used in Section 8 mainly to distinguish the structure to which the word applies in this section from the "Cartesian Product" that is introduced technically as part of the semantics for PAL. Philosophers who may be inclined to balk at phrasing here and there in this work will find it easy enough to substitute amended phrasing consistent with the basic ideas of the work.

Fourth, readers who may be working mathematicians rather than Peirce scholars may find it helpful to know that some of the technical terms involved in the discussions are Peirce's own terms, which are no longer current in mathematics, even though the ideas for which Peirce used the terms are still current. For example, the term "chorisis" would ordinarily be replaced with "pieces" or "separate connected pieces" by graph theorists, who would also replace the term "cyclosis" with "nullity." Topologists would be inclined to replace "chorisis" and "cyclosis," which Peirce called the first two "Listing numbers," with "0-dimensional Betti number" and "1-dimensional Betti number," respectively. And, as has already been mentioned, what Peirce called "Listing's Census Theorem" would ordinarily be said by topologists to be a version of the "Euler-Poincaré Formula."

With these remarks made, we may now enter into the formalism proper of PAL.

The *terms* of PAL comprise three sorts of terms: *primitive terms, elements,* (or: elementary terms), and *arrays.*

Primitive Terms

The *primitive terms* of PAL are terms that are intended to stand for *relations* of all integer adicities $n \geq 1$. (The treatment of adicity 0 will appear in due course.) A primitive term will be written in full as R_i^n, where i is an index from the index set of positive natural numbers, and where n, which is a positive integer, is the adicity of both the term and of any relation for which the term may be understood to stand. PAL is to be understood to possess, for each adicity $n \geq 1$ an infinite number of primitive terms R_1^n, R_2^n, R_3^n, etc. of adicity n. PAL possesses no primitive terms of adicity 0. For primitive terms of adicity 1 the letters P, Q, and N may be used in addition to the letter R. For terms of adicity 2 and greater the letters S, T, and W may be used in addition to the letter R. The term R_i^n in PAL corresponds to what would be written in quantificational logic as

$$R_i(x_1, x_2, \ldots, x_n) \qquad ,$$

with R_i being an indexed relation symbol of adicity n, and the x_i being variable symbols all of which are distinct from each other.

Certain *constant primitive terms* of PAL will be given special symbols. U^1 denotes the "monadic universal relation," $UNIV^1$, which may be understood to mean something like "being self-identical." It corresponds to the relation written in quantificational logic as

$$x = x \quad .$$

U^2, U^3, etc. denote the dyadic universal relation $UNIV^2$, the triadic universal relation $UNIV^3$, etc., respectively, given in quantificational logic as

$$x = x \ \& \ y = y$$

and

$$x = x \ \& \ y = y \ \& \ z = z \quad , \text{etc.,}$$

respectively. 1^2 denotes the dyadic identity relation ID^2, given in quantificational logic as

$$x = y \quad .$$

1^3 denotes the crucially-important triadic identity relation ID^3, called by Peirce "teridentity" and given in quantificational logic as

$$x = y \ \& \ y = z \quad .$$

Similarly, 1^4, 1^5, etc. denote the quadric, pentadic, etc. identity relations, ID^4, ID^5, etc., whose quantificational equivalents are easily understood. There is no primitive term of PAL 1^1. Analogous to the algebraic logic of Bernays, PAL contains null relations. 0^1 denotes the monadic null relation $NULL^1$, given in quantificational logic as

$$x \neq x \quad .$$

0^2, 0^3, etc. denote the dyadic null relation $NULL^2$, the triadic null relation $NULL^3$, etc., respectively, given in quantificational logic as

$$x \neq x \ \& \ y \neq y$$

and

$$x \neq x \ \& \ y \neq y \ \& \ z \neq z \quad , \text{etc.,}$$

respectively.

It should be noted here that there is nothing special about the *particular* formulae of quantificational logic just chosen to indicate relations: if a relation is given by the formula w, it can also be given by any formula logically equivalent to w and containing the same number of distinct free variables as w. Thus, for example, $UNIV^1$ might be given by

  $y = y$;

ID^3 might be given by

  $x = y$ & $x = z$;

and $NULL^2$ might be given by either

  $x \neq x$ & $y = y$

or

  $x \neq x \lor y \neq y$.

Elements

The *elements* of PAL are terms formed from primitive terms by finitely iterated application of certain Peircean *Operations*. These operations are *Negation, Permutation, Join$_1$,* and *Join$_2$*. Join$_1$ and Join$_2$ will be called collectively the *Junction* operations. Unlike primitive terms of PAL, elements of PAL may have adicity 0 as well as positive adicity. Terms of PAL of adicity 0 correspond to the closed sentences of quantificational logic.

The operations of PAL are as follows.

Negation needs no special introduction, except for the symbol used to denote this operation. It will be denoted by NEG, so that, for example, if R_i^n is a primitive term of PAL, then

  $NEG(R_i^n)$

will express the negation of the relation expressed by R_i^n.

In order to understand the various permutation operations, we need first to understand the notion of a "hook," which we might also call an "adicity place." Peirce, in a manner similar to that of Frege, thought of relations as having "unsaturated" positions. It is important that these positions are themselves ordered with respect to each other. Terms for relations, therefore, are also understood to have such ordered positions, and these are called "hooks." In both systems of graphical syntax that are presented in Section 11 of this work, the hooks of the logical terms are actually drawn. In an algebraic logic, like PAL, the hooks need not actually be represented in the symbolism, as long as they are understood to be incorporated into the logic. Now, for any one of the n! permutations of the symmetric group usually written as S_n, say i, there is a corresponding permutation operation

$PERM_i^n$. When, therefore, $PERM_i^n$ is applied to a term of PAL, the result is understood to express the relation that is affiliated with the relation expressed by that term in such a way that the result's hooks are in the order obtained by permuting the hooks of that term in accord with the permutation to which $PERM_i^n$ corresponds, namely i. For example, if $PERM_i^2$ is the operation corresponding to the permutation

$$\begin{pmatrix} 1\,,\,2 \\ 2\,,\,1 \end{pmatrix}\,,$$

and, if R_j^2 is a term that expresses a dyadic relation, then

$$PERM_i^2(R_j^2)$$

is to be understood to express the relation that is the converse relation of the relation expressed by R_j^2. Obviously, the superscript of PERM and that of the term that is its argument must match.

The junction operations are unique to PAL and are the keys to its potential for amalgamating logic with topology. They will be defined more fully further on in this section and in later sections, but some preliminary introduction is useful at the present point. $Join_1$ is to be understood to represent an operation on a single relation of adicity ≥ 2, whereby two of the adicity places of this relation are indicated for a special sort of "selective deletion" (in a sense to be specified further on), and whereby, therefore, a relation is produced that is of adicity 2 less than the relation operated upon. Accordingly, $Join_1$ will be indicated by the symbol

$$J_1^{ij}\,,$$

where the superscripts indicate the adicity places to be "selectively deleted." It may be noted that the superscripts i and j must be such that $i < j$, and $i \geq 1$, while j is no greater than the adicity of the relation on which $Join_1$ is to represent an operation. Accordingly, $Join_1$ is undefined for 0-adic and monadic terms of PAL as argument. $Join_2$ is to be understood to represent an operation on a pair of relations, each of adicity ≥ 1, and taken in a certain order, whereby an adicity place of the first relation and an adicity place of the second relation are indicated for "selective deletion," and whereby a relation is produced that is of adicity 2 less than the *sum* of the adicities of the relations of the pair. Accordingly, $Join_2$ will be indicated by the symbol

$$J_2^{ij}\,,$$

where the superscripts indicate, respectively, the adicity place of the first relation of the pair and (in a way later to be described) the adicity place of the second relation of the pair that are to be "selectively deleted." It should be noted that the superscript i must be both ≥ 1 and yet no greater than the adicity of the first relation of the pair upon which $Join_2$ represents an operation, and that the superscript j must be both strictly greater than the adicity of this first relation and yet not greater than the *sum* of the adicities of both relations in the pair. $Join_2$ is undefined if either member of the pair of terms of PAL that it has as argument is of adicity 0.

The notion of an *element* of PAL may now be made rigorous as follows. An *elementary derivation of an element-candidate t* of PAL is a finite sequence whose last member is t and each member of which is *either*

(1) a primitive term of PAL; *or else*

(2) NEG(E), where E is some previous member of the sequence; *or else*

(3) $PERM_i{}^n(E)$ where E is some previous member of the sequence; *or else*

(4) $J_1{}^{ij}(E)$, where E is some previous member of the sequence; *or else*

(5) $J_2{}^{ij}(E_1,E_2)$, where both E_1 and E_2 are previous members of the sequence.

An *element-candidate t* of PAL is a string of symbols such that there exists some elementary derivation of it.

The *adicity of an element-candidate t* is defined as follows.

(1) If t is a primitive term $R_i{}^n$ then its adicity is n.

(2) If t is NEG(E) then the adicity of t is the adicity of E.

(3) If t is $PERM_i{}^n(E)$, then the adicity of t is the adicity of E.

(4) If t is $J_1{}^{ij}(E)$, then the adicity of t is 2 less than the adicity of E.

(5) If t is $J_2{}^{ij}(E_1,E_2)$, then the adicity of t is 2 less than the sum of the adicities of E_1 and E_2.

An elementary derivation of an element-candidate t of PAL is said to be *consistent with adicity* if and only if:

(1) each occurrence of $PERM_i{}^n(E)$ in it is such that n equals the adicity of E and $1 \leq i \leq n!$;

(2) each occurrence of $J_1{}^{ij}(E)$ in it is such that $1 \leq i < j \leq n$, where n is the adicity of E and $n \geq 2$; and

(3) each occurrence of $J_2^{ij}(E_1,E_2)$ in it is such that $1 \leq i \leq n_1$ and $(n_1+1) \leq j \leq (n_1+n_2)$, where n_1 is the adicity of E_1 and n_2 is the adicity of E_2 and $n_1 \geq 1$ and $n_2 \geq 1$.

Now, we may define an *element* of PAL.

Definition 2.1: An element of PAL is an element-candidate of PAL such that there is an elementary derivation of it that is consistent with adicity.

Because we are not interested in element-candidates that are not elements, we shall henceforth assume that all elementary derivations are consistent with adicity; henceforth, therefore, we shall speak of elementary derivations of elements of PAL. Similarly, we shall henceforth assume that permutation and junction operations spoken of involve subscripts and superscripts that are consistent with adicity.

We may note explicitly here that all primitive terms of PAL are elements of PAL. We may also note that an element E^0 of adicity 0 must either have the form $J_1^{12}(E^2)$, where E^2 is an element of adicity 2, or else have the form $J_2^{12}(E^1,F^1)$, where E^1 and F^1 are both elements of adicity 1.

Before introducing the third sort of term of PAL, *arrays*, six properties possessed by terms need to be discussed. These properties are of importance because the first two of them are connected with the reduction thesis and the last four are connected to Listing's Census Theorem. The properties are *Adicity, Size, Edge Count, Vertex Count, Chorisis,* and *Cyclosis.* These will first be discussed informally.

The *adicity* of a primitive term has already been discussed. The adicity of an element E of PAL is obtained by summing the adicities of all the primitive terms occurrent in E, with each *occurrence* being included in the sum, and then subtracting from this sum twice the number of junction operations occurrent in it. The *size* of an element E is 1 if its adicity is ≥ 1 and is 0 if its adicity is 0. The *edge count* of an element E is the number of junction operations occurrent in it. The *vertex count* of an element E is the number of occurrences of primitive terms in it. The *chorisis* of an element E is always 1. The *cyclosis* of an element E is the number of occurrences of $Join_1$ in it.

More formally, each of the six properties can be defined for elements in a recursive fashion, starting with the primitive terms. For a primitive term R^n of adicity n (note that $n \geq 1$), the properties are as follows:

$$\text{Adicity}(R^n) = n \quad ;$$

$$\text{Size}(R^n) = 1 \quad ;$$

Edges$(R^n) = 0$;

Vertices$(R^n) = 1$;

Chorisis$(R^n) = 1$;

Cyclosis$(R^n) = 0$;

The recursive specification now ensues. Let E be any element of PAL. Then: If F is either NEG(E) or PERM$_i^n$(E), the six properties of F are exactly those of E. If F is J_1^{ij}(E), then

Adicity$(F) = $ Adicity$(E) - 2$;

Size$(F) = 1$ if Adicity$(E) \geq 3$, and

$\qquad = 0$ if Adicity$(E) = 2$;

Edges$(F) = $ Edges$(E) + 1$;

Vertices$(F) = $ Vertices(E) ;

Chorisis$(F) = 1$;

Cyclosis$(F) = $ Cyclosis$(E) + 1$.

Now, let E_1 and E_2 be any two elements (perhaps the same). If F is $J_2^{ij}(E_1, E_2)$, then

Adicity$(F) = $ Adicity$(E_1) + $ Adicity$(E_2) - 2$;

Size$(F) = 1$ if Adicity$(E_1) + $ Adicity$(E_2) \geq 3$, and

$\qquad = 0$ if Adicity$(E_1) + $ Adicity$(E_2) = 2$;

Edges$(F) = $ Edges$(E_1) + $ Edges$(E_2) + 1$;

Vertices$(F) = $ Vertices$(E_1) + $ Vertices(E_2) ;

Chorisis$(F) = 1$; also, Chorisis$(F) = $ Chorisis$(E_1) + $ Chorisis$(E_2) - 1$;

Cyclosis$(F) = $ Cyclosis$(E_1) + $ Cyclosis(E_2) .

We are now in a position to prove two theorems about elements. The first of these relates PAL to Peirce's unified logical vision (ULV). The second of these relates PAL to Listing's topology. Both theorems will subsequently in this work be extended to cover all terms of PAL.

Theorem 2.1 (Valency Rule Theorem for elements of PAL): Let E be an element of PAL; and let n_i be the adicity of the ith occurrence of a primitive term in E, and let e be the edge count of E. Then: if k is the vertex count of E,

$$\text{Adicity}(E) = \left(\sum_{i=1}^{k} n_i \right) - 2e \quad .$$

Proof: The proof is by complete induction on the length of any elementary derivation of E. So, let $E_1, E_2, \ldots, E_m = E$ be any elementary derivation of E. Let us begin by considering the *case m = 1.* In this case, $E = E_1$ and E is thus a primitive term R^n; k = 1 and e = 0. Because the adicity of E is n, and n = n − (2 × 0), the result for this case is proved. Now let us proceed to the *induction step.* Assume that the theorem holds for all elementary derivations of length p, where $1 \le p < m$, so that the theorem is true for all of $E_1, E_2, \ldots, E_p$. We shall show it is true for E_{p+1}. If E_{p+1} is a primitive term, then the theorem holds for it by the same argument used for case m = 1. If E_{p+1} is $NEG(E_i)$ or is $PERM_j^n(E_i)$, for $1 \le i \le p$, then, because by hypothesis the theorem holds for E_i, and because NEG and $PERM_j^n$ leave adicity, edge count, and vertex count unchanged, it follows that the theorem holds for E_{p+1}. If E_{p+1} is $J_1^{rs}(E_i)$ for $1 \le i \le p$, then, because by hypothesis the theorem holds for E_i, and because $Join_1$ reduces adicity by 2 while leaving the sum of the adicities of primitive terms unchanged, leaving k unchanged, and adding 1 to e, it follows that the theorem holds for E_{p+1}. Finally, if E_{p+1} is $J_2^{rs}(E_i, E_j)$ for $1 \le i < j \le p$, then, because by hypothesis the theorem holds for E_i and E_j, and because $Join_2$ reduces the adicity of a sum by 2, we have that:

$$\text{Adicity}(E_{p+1}) = \text{Adicity}(E_i) + \text{Adicity}(E_j) - 2 \quad ,$$

where $\text{Adicity}(E_i)$ and $\text{Adicity}(E_j)$ may be found from the theorem. But, because $Join_2$ adds 1 to the edge count e, and 2 = 2 × 1; and because $Join_2$ leaves the summed vertex count unchanged, the theorem follows for E_{p+1}.

q.e.d.

Theorem 2.2 (Census Theorem for elements of PAL): Let E be an element of PAL, and let e, v, p, and n denote its edge count, vertex count, chorisis, and cyclosis, respectively. Then: $e - v + p - n = 0$.

Proof: The proof is by complete induction on the length of any elementary derivation of E. So, let $E_1, E_2, \ldots, E_m = E$ be an elementary derivation of E. Let us first consider the *case m = 1.* Then $E = E_1$ and E is a primitive term R^n. In this case, e = 0, v = 1, p = 1, and n = 0, so that $e - v + p - n = 0$. Let us now proceed to the induction step. Assume that the theorem holds for all elementary derivations of length k, where $1 \le k < m$, so that the theorem is true for all of E_1, E_2, . . . , E_k. We shall show it is true for E_{k+1}. If E_{k+1} is a primitive term R^n, then the argument for case m = 1 suffices for the result. If E_{k+1} is NEG(E_i) or is $PERM_j^n(E_i)$, for some E_i with $1 \leq i \leq k$, then, because the theorem holds for E_i and because NEG and $PERM_j^n$ leave e, v, p, and n unchanged, the result follows at once for E_{k+1}. If E_{k+1} is $J_1^{rs}(E_i)$, for $1 \leq i \leq k$, then, because by hypothesis the theorem holds for E_i, and because $Join_1$ changes e by +1, changes v by 0, changes p by 0, and changes n by + 1, $Join_1$ changes e − v + p − n by 1 − 0 + 0 − 1 = 0; and thus the value for E_{k+1} is the same as the value for E_i, namely 0. Thus the result follows for E_{k+1}. If E_{k+1} is $J_2^{rs}(E_i, E_j)$, for $1 \leq i < j \leq k$, then because by hypothesis the theorem is true for E_i and E_j, we have the following. (Indices are used here in the obvious way.)

$$e_{k+1} = e_i + e_j + 1 \quad ;$$
$$v_{k+1} = v_i + v_j \quad ;$$
$$p_{k+1} = p_i + p_j - 1 \quad ;$$
$$n_{k+1} = n_i + n_j \quad ;$$

Thus,

$$(e - v + p - n)_{k+1} = (e - v + p - n)_i + (e - v + p - n)_j + 1 - 1$$
$$= 0 + 0 + 0$$
$$= 0 \quad .$$

And the result follows for E_{k+1}.

q.e.d.

Corollary 2.2.1: If E is any element of PAL, and e, v, and n are as in the theorem, then n = e − v + 1.

Proof: For any element E, p = 1, so that e − v + 1 − n = 0. The result follows immediately.

q.e.d.

ARRAYS

We may now proceed to define the third sort of term of PAL, *arrays*. *Definition 2.2:* Let $\xi = \{E_1, E_2, . . . , E_n\}$ be a set of distinct elements of PAL of arbitrary adicities, including perhaps also elements of adicity 0. Then, *an array of PAL consisting of elements of* ξ is a finite sequence of length $k \geq 1$, each of whose entries is an element of ξ. If α is an array *consisting of* elements of ξ, *and* if each element of ξ occurs as an entry in α at least once, then α will be said to be an array *of* ξ. To avoid unnecessarily cumbersome terminology, an array of length 1 will be spoken of simply as *being* an element of PAL, and an element of PAL will be spoken of as simply *being* an array of length 1.

Arrays may be written in either of two ways. *First*, we may place the array inside parentheses, with each entry of an element in the array separated from the other entries by commas; this fashion of writing arrays duplicates one familiar manner of writing ordered n-tuples. Thus, an array consisting of elements of the set $\{R^0, R^2, J_1^{23}(S^4)\}$ might be written, for example, as

$(R^2, R^2, J_1^{23}(S^4), R^2, J_1^{23}(S^4), R^0)$.

This would be an array with one entry of R^0, three entries of R^2, and two entries of $J_1^{23}(S^4)$. *Second*, and preferably, arrays may be written in the "Zusammenfügung" notation of Bernays, with a small circle denoting the "Zusammenfügung" operation. Because the operation is associative, parentheses can be omitted. In "Zusammenfügung" notation, the above array would be written as

$R^2 \circ R^2 \circ J_1^{23}(S^4) \circ R^2 \circ J_1^{23}(S^4) \circ R^0$.

If α is any array of PAL, then α will be said to *retract to* an array β. The array β, will be said to be *the result of retracting* α. If α is an array having at least one entry of a 0-adic element *and* at least one entry of an n-adic element for $n \geq 1$, then the result of retracting α, namely β, results from α by extracting from α all the entries of 0-adic elements in it and shortening its length (that is, its chorisis) accordingly. If α has no entries of 0-adic elements occurring in it, then the result of retracting α is α itself. If α either has no 0-adic elements occurring as entries or has at least one 0-adic *and* at least one n-adic element, for $n \geq 1$, occurring in it, then β, the result of retracting α, will have no 0-adic elements occurring as entries in it. Thus, for example, the array

$P^1 \circ R^2$

is the result of retracting the array

$P^1 \circ R^2$

itself, as it is also the result of retracting the array

$E^0 \circ P^1 \circ F^0 \circ F^0 \circ R^2 \circ E^0 \circ E^0 \circ F^0 \circ F^0$,

and the result of retracting the array

$E^0 \circ F^0 \circ P^1 \circ E^0 \circ R^2 \circ F^0$,

and so forth. If α is an array *all of whose entries* are elements of adicity 0, then the result of retracting α is α itself. The result β of retracting α differs from α if and only if α is an array containing both entries of adicity 0 and entries of adicity more than 0.

The notions of adicity, size, edge count, vertex count, chorisis, and cyclosis may now be extended so as to be applicable to arrays of PAL. We could define the chorisis of an array to be simply its length, because an array is a finite sequence. Alternatively, the chorisis of an array can be defined as the *sum* of the chorises of all the entries of elements in it, because the chorisis of each occurrence of an element is 1. Now this idea of *summing* over all the entries of elements in an array is one by means of which we may attach to any array, not only a chorisis, but also an adicity, a size, an edge count, a vertex count, and a cyclosis.

Specifically, let $(E_1, E_2, \ldots, E_n)$ be an array of elements, with each E_i here being an entry of an element. Let us call this array α.

Then we may institute the following definitions:

$$\text{Adicity}(\alpha) = \sum_{i=1}^{n} \text{Adicity}(E_i) \quad ;$$

$$\text{Size}(\alpha) = \sum_{i=1}^{n} \text{Size}(E_i) \quad ;$$

$$\text{Edges}(\alpha) = \sum_{i=1}^{n} \text{Edges}(E_i) \quad ;$$

$$\text{Vertices}(\alpha) = \sum_{i=1}^{n} \text{Vertices}(E_i) \quad ;$$

$$\text{Chorisis}(\alpha) = \sum_{i=1}^{n} \text{Chorisis}(E_i) = n \quad ;$$

$$\text{Cyclosis}(\alpha) = \sum_{i=1}^{n} \text{Cyclosis}(E_i) \quad .$$

Let us take note here again that arrays of PAL of chorisis 1 (that is, length 1) and single elements of PAL will be regarded simply as *being the same thing*.

It is useful to see how retracting an array affects these properties. In order to do this let us review an example previously given, namely the array

$$P^1 \circ R^2 \quad ,$$

which is the result of retracting the array

$$E^0 \circ P^1 \circ F^0 \circ F^0 \circ R^2 \circ E^0 \circ E^0 \circ F^0 \circ F^0 \quad ,$$

and also the result of retracting the array

$$E^0 \circ F^0 \circ P^1 \circ E^0 \circ R^2 \circ F^0 \quad .$$

We may note in this case that, although the chorisis of each of these three arrays differs from that of each of the others, adicity and size is the same for all three. In general, retracting preserves both adicity and size. Retracting does not in general preserve edge count, vertex count, chorisis, or cyclosis.

Although this completes the introduction of the three sorts of *terms* of PAL, it is necessary at this point to introduce an additional structural notion of PAL: an *Assembly*. Assemblies are crucial in connecting PAL with topology by means of graphical syntaxes. The notion of an assembly, moreover, is fundamental for Peirce's notion of construction and hence his notion of reduction. We now, therefore, proceed to introduce the notion of an assembly.

On the set of arrays consisting of elements of (a set of elements) ξ, we define an equivalence relation $\approx$ by letting $\alpha \approx \beta$ if and only if: for all E_i in ξ, E_i occurs as an entry exactly j times in α if and only if E_i occurs as an entry exactly j times in β. This equivalence relation partitions the set of arrays consisting of elements of ξ into equivalence classes. Each such equivalence class will be called *an assembly consisting of elements of* ξ. In every array α in any given assembly A consisting of elements of ξ, any given element E_i in ξ will occur as an entry the same number of times, perhaps 0. The number of times that E_i occurs as an entry in any array in A will be called the number of times that E_i occurs as an entry *in the assembly A*. If each E_i in ξ occurs as an entry in the assembly A at least once, then A will be called an assembly *of* elements of ξ.

It is obvious that any two arrays in the same assembly A have the same adicity, the same size, the same edge count, the same vertex count, the same chorisis, and the same cyclosis. Thus we may define the adicity of an assembly A to be the adicity of any array α in it, the size of an assembly A to be the size of any array α in it, and similarly for the edge count, the vertex count, the chorisis, and the cyclosis. In this way we immediately extend the applicability of these six notions from arrays to assemblies.

Any assembly A consisting of elements of ξ is simply an equivalence class, whose members are mutually equivalent arrays (where "equivalent" refers to the equivalence relation $\approx$). If A has chorisis k, then any array in A is simply a sequence of length k of elements E_i in ξ, with each element E_i in ξ occurring in the sequence the exact number of times (perhaps 0) that it occurs as an entry in A. We may, therefore, think of assemblies of elements as being something like "unordered sequences of elements," or as being something like "sets" of elements, where "sets" may contain repeated occurrences of the same element. (Theoretical computer scientists sometimes use the word "bag" to capture this idea.) In general, if an assembly A is of chorisis k; and if $E_{i(1)}$, $E_{i(2)}$, . . . ,$E_{i(m)}$ are the elements of ξ that occur at least once as an entry in A, with each $E_{i(j)}$ occurring as an entry in A exactly n_j times; then we have that the number of distinct arrays in A is given by the formula:

$$\frac{k!}{n_1! \, n_2! \, \ldots \, n_m!} \quad .$$

We may write assemblies of elements by adopting a square bracket notation similar to the curly bracket notation that is used to denote sets, and by allowing inscriptions between the square brackets to be repeated. Thus,

$$[E_{i(1)}, E_{i(1)}, \ldots, E_{i(1)}, E_{i(2)}, E_{i(2)}, \ldots, E_{i(2)}, \ldots,$$
$$E_{i(m)}, E_{i(m)}, \ldots, E_{i(m)}] \quad ,$$

where $E_{i(j)}$ occurs n_j times, would represent an assembly in which each element $E_{i(j)}$ has n_j entries. In such a representation of assemblies, the order of the entries of elements is not of any particular consequence. We might wish, however, to represent an assembly by picking some *canonical* array to represent it; and a good choice for such a canonical array would be the array corresponding to the order in which the representation just above has been given. According to it, all entries of multiply-occurrent elements E_i are grouped together, and then the groups are placed in order in accord with some previously established order in ξ.

Theorem 2.1 and Theorem 2.2 may now be extended to arrays and assemblies.

Theorem 2.3 (Valency Rule Theorem for Arrays and Assemblies of PAL): Let A be any assembly of elements of PAL and α any array in A. Furthermore, let n_i be the adicity of the ith occurrence as an entry of a primitive term in A as ordered in α; let e be the edge count of A (equivalently: of α); and let k be the vertex count of A (equivalently: of α). Then, the adicity of A (equivalently: the adicity of α) is given by

$$\text{Adicity}(A) = \left(\sum_{i=1}^{k} n_i \right) - 2e \quad .$$

Proof: In virtue of Theorem 1 and the fact that the adicity of A, the edge count of A, and the vertex count of A (equivalently: of α) are all obtained simply by summing over all occurrences as entries of elements in A, the proof is obvious.

                                                                                q.e.d.

Theorem 2.4 (Census Theorem for Arrays and Assemblies of PAL): Let A be any assembly of elements of PAL and α any array in A. Furthermore, let e, v, p, and n denote the edge count, vertex count, chorisis, and cyclosis, respectively of A (equivalently: of α). Then: $e - v + p - n = 0$.

Proof: In virtue of Theorem 2 and the fact that the edge count, vertex count, chorisis, and cyclosis of A (equivalently: of α) are all obtained by summing over all occurrences as entries of elements in A, the proof is obvious.

                                                                                q.e.d.

The terms of PAL, as was said at the beginning of this section, are intended to "stand for" relations. The meaning of this "standing for" will be explicated exactly in the following two sections of this work. In the present section, nevertheless, it is of value for the purpose of understanding the operations of PAL to give a few informal preliminaries about how the terms of PAL "stand for" relations. Readers who find exact exposition more valuable than heuristics, or who find informal explication confusing, may wish at this point to skip directly to Section 3.

It will be said that the terms of PAL both *express* relations and *represent* relations, where these two notions are slightly different. It is to be understood that each term of PAL always both expresses a relation and represents a relation whose adicity in each case is the adicity of that term. Moreover, the constant terms of PAL, namely U^n, 1^n, and 0^n, will be said to *denote* relations. The arrays of PAL will also be said to *depict* sequences of relations, in a manner that will be explicated in Section 3 and Section 4. The way in which terms of PAL express and represent relations will now be discussed in a partial, informal, and preliminary fashion. (In Section 3 and Section 4 of this work, the notions of expression, representation, and depiction will be explicated exactly.)

A *primitive term* $R_i{}^n$ of PAL will be said to *express directly* a relation of adicity n. An *element* F of PAL will be said to express a relation in accord with the following recursive schema:

(1) If F is NEG(E), then F will express the relation that is *the complement* of the relation expressed by E. Negation was discussed earlier in this work.

(2) If F is $PERM_i{}^n(E)$, then F will express the relation that is *the ith permutation* (of the symmetric group usually written as S_n) of the relation expressed by E. Permutation was discussed earlier in this work.

(3) If F is $J_1{}^{ij}(E)$, then F will express the relation that is *the ij^{th} $Join_1$* of the relation expressed by E. $Join_1$ will be discussed immediately below.

(4) If F is $J_2{}^{ij}(E_1, E_2)$, then F will express the relation that is *the ij^{th} $Join_2$* of the relations expressed by E_1 and E_2, in that order. $Join_2$ will be discussed immediately below.

We may now begin to understand further the connection between the relation expressed by an application of one of the junction operations and the relation or relations expressed by the argument or arguments of such an application. Let us begin with $Join_1$. Let E^n be an element of adicity $n \geq 2$; and let the relation expressed by E^n be given in quantificational logic as

$$R^n(x_1, x_2, \ldots, x_n) \quad ,$$

where, of course, all the variables are distinct. Now, let i,j be such that $1 \leq i < j \leq n$. Then the element

$$J_1{}^{ij}(E^n)$$

will express the relation given in quantificational logic as

$$(\exists y) R^n(x_1, \ldots, x_{i-1}, y, x_{i+1}, \ldots, x_{j-1}, y, x_{j+1}, \ldots, x_n) \ .$$

In effect, therefore, $Join_1$ identifies the ith and j^{th} adicity places in the relation expressed by E^n, and then quantifies existentially with respect to these places. If E^n is such that n = 2, so that E^n expresses a relation of adicity 2, then $J_1{}^{ij}(E^n)$ will express the 0-adic relation: Something has to itself the relation expressed by E^n.

Now let us consider $Join_2$. Let an element $E_1{}^n$ and an element $E_2{}^m$ be given, with $n \geq 1$ and $m \geq 1$; and let $E_1{}^n$ and $E_2{}^m$ be such that they express, respectively, the relations given in quantificational logic as

$\qquad R^n(x_1, x_2, \ldots, x_n)$

and

$\qquad S^m(y_1, y_2, \ldots, y_m)$,

where all the variables in the above two lines are distinct from one another. Also, let i,j be such that $1 \leq i \leq n$ and $(n + 1) \leq j \leq (n + m)$. Then the element

$\qquad J_2{}^{ij}(E_1{}^n, E_2{}^m)$

will express the relation given in quantificational logic as

$\qquad (\exists z)\,[\,R^n(x_1, \ldots, x_{i-1}, z, x_{i+1}, \ldots, x_n)\ \&\ S^m(y_1, \ldots, y_{j-n-1}, z, y_{j-n+1}, \ldots, y_m)\,]$.

In effect, therefore, $Join_2$ conjoins two relations, ensuring in this conjunction that all adicity places involved are kept distinct; *then* identifies the ith adicity place of the first conjunct with the $(j - n)^{th}$ adicity place of the second conjunct; *and then* quantifies existentially with respect to these two places. If $E_1{}^n$ and $E_2{}^m$ are such that $n = m = 1$, so that both $E_1{}^n$ and $E_2{}^m$ express relations of adicity 1, then $J_2{}^{12}(E_1{}^n, E_2{}^m)$ will express the 0-adic relation: Something has *both* the relation (property) expressed by $E_1{}^n$ *and* the relation (property) expressed by $E_2{}^m$.

Readers may wish to take note here of the fact that $Join_1$ may be defined in terms of the permutations and Herzberger's bonding operation, and that $Join_2$ may be defined in terms of the permutations and the relative product operation. Readers may also wish to note that the intuitive topological or graph-theoretical meaning of the junction operations is this: they join, or bond together, what we may call two "loose ends," "unfilled adicity places," "valental positions," or (to use Frege's terminology) "unsaturated positions" in relations. $Join_1$ connects two "loose ends" in a single relation of adicity ≥ 2, yielding a relation of adicity 2 less than the relation so operated upon. $Join_2$ connects a "loose end" of one relation of adicity ≥ 1 with a "loose end" of another relation of adicity ≥ 1, yielding as a result a relation of adicity 2 less than the sum of the adicities of the two relations so operated upon.

Now that we have seen in a preliminary way how primitive terms and elements of PAL express relations, we are ready to turn to *arrays*. An array of

PAL of chorisis 1 will be said to express the relation expressed by the element that has a single occurrence in the array, which in this work is being regarded as simply identical with the array of chorisis 1 itself. An array of chorisis greater than 1, none of whose entries is an element of adicity 0, will be said to express the relation that in quantificational logic would be given by *conjoining*, in the order determined by the array, the quantificational equivalents of all the occurrences of elements in the array, with care being taken to ensure that all occurrences of *free* variables in the conjunction are occurrences of *distinct* variables, so that each free variable in the conjunction occurs exactly once. For example, if

$$(P^1, R^2, P^1, P^1, R^2)$$

is an array consisting of elements of the set $\{P^1, R^2\}$; and if P^1 is given in quantificational logic by $P(x_1)$; and if R_2 is given in quantificational logic by $R(x_1, x_2)$; then the relation this array expresses is given in quantificational logic as

$$P(x_1) \ \& \ R(x_2, x_3) \ \& \ P(x_4) \ \& \ P(x_5) \ \& \ R(x_6, x_7) \quad .$$

Arrays of chorisis greater than 1, some or all of whose entries are occurrences of elements of adicity 0 express relations in a slightly more complicated fashion. If such an array has at least one entry of adicity ≥ 1, then the relation expressed by the array is the relation expressed by the result of retracting it. An array *all* of whose entries are of adicity 0 will express a relation in a manner that will be specified in Sections 3 and 4 of this work.

It should be noted again here that the adicity of the relation expressed by an array and the adicity of the relation represented by an array are the same, and that this is the adicity of the array itself.

By contrast with arrays, which express and represent (single) relations, assemblies of PAL do not in general express or represent (single) relations. Rather, assemblies *potentially express* relations and *potentially represent* relations by comprising a collection of arrays, each one of which does express a (single) relation and does represent a (single) relation.

Now that the *terms* of PAL have been introduced, we may proceed briefly to introduce the fact that there are *well-formed formulae of PAL*. The basic or primitive formula of PAL connects two terms t_1 and t_2 of PAL with the sign = , thus:

$$t_1 = t_2 \quad .$$

The formula is read as "t_1 and t_2 subsume each other." The idea that one relation is subsumed by or is part of another is intuitively given in the way that, for example, the relation "being a brother of _____" is subsumed by the relation "being a sibling of _____", which is in turn subsumed by the relation "being a familial relative of _____", and so forth. Except for this remark and two brief points in the following two sections, the whole topic of the well-formed formulae of PAL, as well as their significance, must be reserved for a future work.

3

SEMANTICS FOR PEIRCEAN ALGEBRAIC LOGIC,
PART ONE

The presentation of the full intensional semantics for PAL will be accomplished in two stages. In this section, the first stage will be presented; it is an extensional semantics, in the sense that in this stage the terms of PAL are interpreted as "classes of n-tuples" over a domain D that is a set. The concept of a "class of n-tuples" differs from the usual concept of a set of n-tuples, although the two concepts are closely affiliated.

For the extensional semantics that will be developed in this section we shall need a background set theory. It is more or less arbitrary which of the standard set theories we specify as background. Let us, however, for the sake of definiteness, accept as our background set theory ZFC, that is, Zermelo-Fraenkel set theory plus the axiom of choice. Gödel-von Neumann-Bernays set theory would work equally well. An interpretation in the extensional sense, which will be called an *Enterpretation*, will be distinguished from an interpretation in the intensional sense, which will be called an *Interpretation*. An Enterpretation of PAL will be regarded as a pair (D,*), with D being a certain sort of set and with * being a function from terms of PAL to finite sequences of what will be called "classes of n-tuples" over D, with * satisfying certain conditions. * will be called an Enterpretation function. The notion of "a class of n-tuples" employed differs from the standard notion of a class of n-tuples, in a manner that will be explicated in this section.

In the second stage of presentation of the full intensional semantics for PAL, which will be accomplished in the following section of this work, the ideas of the present section will be extended. The goal is to make the full semantics for PAL as intensional as it seems feasible to do consistent with precision. This is done by introducing the notion of a "relation-simpliciter." "Relations-simpliciter" are defined by appealing to a structure similar to the Kripke structures that are the staples of modal semantics. (Indeed, although modal-logical apparatus will not be developed for PAL in this work, it should be evident from the intensional semantics how one might proceed to add modal structure to PAL.) An Interpretation (that is, an interpretation in the intensional sense) of PAL will emerge as a assignment to each term of PAL, of a sequence of "relations-simpliciter," with the assignment satisfying certain conditions analogous to those that the functions

27

* of Enterpretations satisfy. Let us, therefore, proceed straightway to the extensional semantics for PAL and to the notion of an Enterpretation.

In order to explicate the first stage of the semantics for PAL, we presuppose the natural numbers 1, 2, 3, etc., as well as the background set theory ZFC. We also employ the notion of a function, as follows. A function $f: S \to S'$ from the non-empty set S to the non-empty set S' is a set of ordered pairs (s,s') such that s is a member of S and s' is a member of S'; such that, if (s,s'_1) and (s,s'_2) are both members of f, then $s'_1 = s'_2$; and such that for all s in S there exists some (s,s') in f.

The semantics for PAL also presupposes that there are two "truth values," namely "the value true," written as T, and "the value false," written as $\perp$. The two truth values are to be accepted as primitively given "classes of 0-tuples" in the semantics for PAL; and it is to be accepted that there are no other primitively given "classes of 0-tuples." A *domain of Enterpretation D for PAL* is any non-empty set not containing either of the truth values.

Given the idea of a domain of Enterpretation D for PAL, we now proceed to define the notion of tuples over D in a manner slightly different from the usual one. We also define a special notion of a *class of n-tuples over D*, and it is to be noted again that the notion of such "classes" is not to be confused with the notion of sets in general but is rather a technically defined notion.

Given any domain of Enterpretation D for PAL, we define for $n \geq 1$ an *n-sequence on D* to be a function from the set of natural numbers $\{1,2,\ldots,n\}$ to D. We then define for $n \geq 1$ an *n-tuple over D* to be a function f from the set $S^n(D)$ of all n-sequences on D to the set $\{\mathsf{T},\perp\}$ such that *for at most one* s in $S^n(D)$, $f(s) = \mathsf{T}$. An n-tuple f over D such that there is *exactly one* s in $S^n(D)$ with $f(s) = \mathsf{T}$ will be written as that one n-sequence s itself might be written, namely as a framed list of n (not necessarily distinct) members of D. This manner of writing such an n-tuple over D duplicates the familiar representation of an n-tuple over D as the notion is ordinarily defined, thus:

$$(d_1, d_2, \ldots, d_n) \quad .$$

The (obviously unique) n-tuple f over D such that for all s in $S^n(D)$ $f(s) = \perp$ will be written as

$$(, , \ldots ,) \quad , \text{ with n blank places,}$$

or, for short as

$$( )^n \quad .$$

It is called *the null n-tuple over D*. A *tuple over D* is any n-tuple over D for any integer n ≥ 1.

In terms of the two truth values T and ⊥, and the notion of an n-tuple over D for n ≥ 1, we may now define for n ≥ 0 the technical notion of a *class of n-tuples over D*.

Definition 3.1: For any domain of Enterpretation D, the truth values T and ⊥ will be said to be, by definition, *the two classes of 0-tuples over D*. (There are no other classes of 0-tuples.) Moreover, for n ≥ 1, a *class X^n of n-tuples over D* is a *set* of n-tuples over D (as defined above) such that either X^n *contains only* the null n-tuple or else *does not contain* the null n-tuple.

By the "adicity" of a class of n-tuples is meant simply the number n.

Classes of n-tuples for n ≥ 1 will also be called *matrices* of n-tuples. The justification for this convention is that, when classes of n-tuples other than the truth values are written out with each n-tuple being written below a previous one, starting from some given n-tuple, a matrix of values from D, or of blanks, results. Once an ordering of a domain D is fixed—which, given the axiom of choice and thus the well-ordering theorem, is always possible—the order of the n-tuples in a given class of n-tuples over D may be canonically specified by means of a lexicographical ordering. In the finite case, the matrix may be completely written out, thus:

$$\begin{Bmatrix} (d_{11}, d_{12}, \ldots, d_{1n}) \\ (d_{21}, d_{22}, \ldots, d_{2n}) \\ \cdots\cdots\cdots\cdots\cdots \\ (d_{k1}, d_{k2}, \ldots, d_{kn}) \end{Bmatrix} \quad .$$

In the infinite case, for n ≥ 1, we may still speak of a matrix in place of speaking of a class of n-tuples, by extension.

With a view to the matrix in question, we may speak of the "columns" of a class (or: matrix) of n-tuples over D, for n ≥ 1. We may consider each such column as a "column vector," and thus introduce column vector notation to present classes of n-tuples. Thus, if δ_i denotes the ith column vector in a class of n-tuples over D, we may represent this class of n-tuples as

$$\{(\delta_1, \delta_2, \ldots, \delta_n)\} \quad .$$

We may now define a *block* of a matrix of n-tuples to be any submatrix of it that consists of any k pairwise adjacent columns (or: column vectors) of it. Thus, for example,

$$\{(\delta_1, \delta_2, \delta_3)\}$$

is a block of the original matrix above. Because there will, in general, be rows that are duplicates of each other in such blocks, we will not be able *simply* to speak of blocks as corresponding to classes of n-tuples. But we may achieve this correspondence by eliminating duplicate rows and re-ordering the rows lexicographically in accord with the order fixed on D.

In general, the symbols X_i^n, Y_i^n, and W_i^n will be used to denote classes of n-tuples for $n \geq 1$. Additionally, certain special symbols will be used to denote certain special classes of n-tuples. We have already seen, of course, the symbols T and $\perp$, that are used to denote the two classes of 0-tuples, the truth values. Also, for $n \geq 1$, V^n denotes the *universal class* of n-tuples over D, that is the set of all n-tuples over D *except* the null n-tuple. For $n \geq 1$, Z^n denotes the *zero class* of n-tuples over D, that is the set containing *only* the null n-tuple. For $n \geq 2$, I^n denotes the *identity class* of n-tuples over D, that is the set of all n-tuples over D, *excluding* the null n-tuple, in which *every* entry of any given n-tuple is the *same* member of D. It is also allowable to use the symbol V^0 in place of the symbol T and to use the symbol Z^0 in place of the symbol $\perp$. We do not require the symbol I^1 because V^1 already provides for the role I^1 would have, and because having such a symbol would invite confusion: for I^n is not V^n in general.

Crucial in the semantics for PAL are finite sequences of classes of n-tuples over a domain D. Analogously to the manner in which arrays of PAL are written, sequences of classes of n-tuples will be written using a symbol for an operation. The symbol employed will be the same symbol used to write arrays, namely $\circ$. Thus the sequence $(X^1, \mathsf{T}, Y^5, \mathsf{T}, \perp)$, for example, may also be written as

$$X^1 \circ \mathsf{T} \circ Y^5 \circ \mathsf{T} \circ \perp \quad .$$

A sequence of classes of n-tuples over D *of length 1*, and the single class of n-tuples over D that is the entry of that sequence, will be regarded as being simply *the same thing*; this convention is the same one that was adopted in the previous section for arrays.

By the "adicity" of a sequence of classes of n-tuples is meant simply the *sum* of the adicities of all the entries in the sequence.

Analogous to the notion of *retracting* an array of PAL, there is the notion of retracting a sequence of classes of n-tuples. For instance, the result of retracting the example given just above is the sequence of classes of n-tuples

$$X^1 \circ Y^5 \quad .$$

In order to define retraction in general in the case of sequences of classes of n-tuples, we will need to introduce an operator CP (for "Cartesian Product") on such sequences. This operator and the definition of retraction for such sequences will be defined further on in this section.

The semantics for PAL requires four types of operations on classes of n-tuples over a domain D: *complementation, permutations*, a *"Cartesian Product,"* and *selective double deletion*. These will now be explained.

The *complement* of a class X^n of n-tuples over D will be written as $\langle X^n \rangle$ For all $n \geq 1$, if X^n is neither V^n nor Z^n, then $\langle X^n \rangle$ is the set of all n-tuples, *excluding* the null n-tuple, that are not members of X^n. For all $n \geq 1$, $\langle V^n \rangle = Z^n$ and $\langle Z^n \rangle = V^n$. $\langle T \rangle = \perp$ and $\langle \perp \rangle = T$.

The *permutation* operations operate columnwise on matrices of n-tuples over a domain D. Let X^n be the class (matrix) of n-tuples

$$\{(\delta_1, \delta_2, \ldots, \delta_n)\} \quad .$$

And let P_i^n be the *inverse* of the permutation

$$\begin{pmatrix} 1, & 2, & \ldots, & n \\ p(1), & p(2), & \ldots, & p(n) \end{pmatrix} \quad ,$$

which places whatever is in position 1 into position $p(1)$, whatever is in position 2 into position $p(2)$, and so forth. That is to say, let P_i^n be the permutation

$$\begin{pmatrix} p(1), & p(2), & \ldots, & p(n) \\ 1, & 2, & \ldots, & n \end{pmatrix} \quad ,$$

which places whatever is in position $p(1)$ into position 1, whatever is in position $p(2)$ into position 2, and so forth. Then $P_i^n(X^n)$ is the class (matrix) of n-tuples

$$\{(\delta_{p(1)}, \delta_{p(2)}, \ldots, \delta_{p(n)})\} \quad .$$

Permutations do not apply, or apply only trivially, to the truth values and to classes of l-tuples, leaving them unchanged. Applied to the Z^n, the permutations also leave them unchanged.

The *"Cartesian Product"* of a class X^n of n-tuples over D and a class Y^m of m-tuples over D is defined in a manner slightly different from the usual one; but it is written, in the usual fashion, as $X^n \times Y^m$. For $n \geq 1$ and $m \geq 1$ and $X^n \neq Z^n$ and $Y^m \neq Z^m$, $X^n \times Y^m$ is the set of all $(n + m)$-tuples

$$(d_1^x, d_2^x, \ldots, d_n^x, d_1^y, d_2^y, \ldots, d_m^y)$$

over D with $(d_1^x, d_2^x, \ldots, d_n^x)$ a member of X^n and $(d_1^y, d_2^y, \ldots, d_m^y)$ a member of Y^m. For all X^n with $n \geq 1$ and for all $m \geq 1$, we have that

$$X^n \times Z^m = Z^m \times X^n = Z^{n+m} \quad .$$

The truth value T acts as a sort of "unit" or "identity" element with respect to "Cartesian Product." That is, for all X^n with $n \geq 1$, we have that

$$X^n \times \mathsf{T} = \mathsf{T} \times X^n = X^n \quad .$$

Furthermore,

$$\mathsf{T} \times \mathsf{T} = \mathsf{T} , \text{ and } \mathsf{T} \times \bot = \bot \times \mathsf{T} = \bot \quad .$$

So, more generally, we can say that, for all X^n with $n \geq 0$, we have that $X^n \times \mathsf{T} = \mathsf{T} \times X^n = X^n$. The truth value $\bot$ acts as a sort of "zero" element with respect to "Cartesian Product." That is, for all X^n with $n \geq 1$, we have that

$$X^n \times \bot = \bot \times X^n = Z^n \quad .$$

Furthermore,

$$\mathsf{T} \times \bot = \bot \times \mathsf{T} = \bot \times \bot = \bot \quad .$$

So, more generally, we can say that for all X^n with $n \geq 0$, we have that $X^n \times \bot = \bot \times X^n = Z^n$. Henceforth in this work, "Cartesian Product" will be written without the surrounding quotation marks.

Cartesian Products may, in the usual way, be formed from any finite number of classes of n-tuples. It is easily verified that Cartesian Product is associative; we need not, therefore, worry about parentheses in writing multiple Cartesian Products. Each class of n-tuples that goes into the formation of a Cartesian Product may be called a Cartesian Factor of that Product. The Cartesian Product is always a class of k-tuples where k is the sum of the adicities of all the classes of n-tuples that are factors of the Product.

Given the Cartesian Product operation as just defined, we may now define an operator CP on finite sequences of classes of n-tuples over a domain D, as follows. Let $s = X_1^{n_1} \circ X_2^{n_2} \circ \ldots \circ X_k^{n_k}$ be such a sequence. Then CP(s) is the Cartesian Product

$$X_1^{n_1} \times X_2^{n_2} \times \ldots \times X_k^{n_k} \quad .$$

The operator CP simply replaces each occurrence of the symbol $\circ$ in a sequence with the operator for Cartesian Product. (If s is a sequence of length 1, that is, is a single class of n-tuples, then CP(s) = s.)

With the operator CP on sequences of classes of n-tuples over a domain D thus defined, we may now define the notion of retraction for such sequences. Indeed, we define a retraction operator Ret on such sequences.

Definition 3.2: Let s be any finite sequence of classes of n-tuples over a domain D. Then we define *the retraction of s, Ret(s)*, as follows:

(1) If s has *no* classes of 0-tuples (that is, truth values) occurring as entries in it, then $Ret(s) = s$;

(2) If s has *only* classes of 0-tuples occurring as entries in it, then $Ret(s) = CP(s)$; that is, $Ret(s) = \mathsf{T}$ if all entries in s are entries of T, and $Ret(s) = \bot$ if some entry in s is $\bot$;

(3) If s has at least one entry that is a class of 0-tuples *and* at least one entry that is a class of n-tuples for $n \geq 1$, then $Ret(s)$ is the sequence of classes of n-tuples obtained from s by extracting from it all entries that are classes of 0-tuples and then shortening its length accordingly.

For Cartesian Products not involving the truth values, we may define the notion of blocks corresponding to factors. For example, for $n \geq 1$ and $m \geq 1$, we may define *the block of $X^n \times Y^m$ corresponding to the factor X^n* to be the first n columns (column-vectors) of this Cartesian Product. Similarly, we may define the block of the product corresponding to the factor Y^m to be the last m columns (column-vectors) of the Product.

We may, therefore, easily extend this idea to *multiple* Cartesian Products not involving the truth values, that is to say those with three or more factors, all of which have adicity ≥ 1. If $n_i \geq 1$ for all i with $1 \leq i \leq m$,

$$X_1^{n_1} \times X_2^{n_2} \times \ldots \times X_m^{n_m}$$

is a given multiple Cartesian Product, then the block corresponding to the factor $X_k^{n_k}$ is all the columns (column-vectors) numbered from

$$\sum_{i=1}^{k-1} n_i \; + 1$$

to

$$\sum_{i=1}^{k} n_i \quad .$$

Selective Double Deletion, which will be written as SD, is a collection of operations that can be applied only to classes of n-tuples X^n for $n \geq 2$. SD may be defined in terms of the permutations and the "Streichung" operation of Bernays, but in the context of PAL it is most appropriately defined as follows. Let X^n be any class of n-tuples over D with $n \geq 2$. And let i, j be integers such that $1 \leq i < j \leq n$. Then the ij^{th} Selective Double Deletion applied to X^n, which is written as

$$SD^{ij}(X^n)$$

or as

$$SD^{i,j}(X^n) \quad ,$$

is the class of all $(n - 2)$-tuples over D that are formed from X^n by *first* selecting from X^n all of its n-tuples that contain the same member of D in both the ith and j^{th} positions, and then *secondly* deleting from each of these selected n-tuples both the ith and j^{th} entries and then "closing up" to form an $(n - 2)$-tuple.

We may make this explanation more exact as follows: We define two collections of operations on classes of n-tuples. The first is the collection of *selection* operations SEL^{ij} and the second is the collection of *double-deletion* operations DEL^{ij}. (As with SD, SEL and DEL may be written with commas separating the superscripts as necessary for readability.) Both are defined for arguments X^n, with $n \geq 2$, and for $1 \leq i < j \leq n$. $SEL^{ij}(X^n)$ is the class of all n-tuples in X^n that contain the same member of D in both the ith and the jth places. If no n-tuple in X^n has the same member of D in both the ith and j^{th} places, then $SEL^{ij}(X^n) = Z^n$, the class containing only the null n-tuple. Moreover, $SEL^{ij}(Z^n) = Z^n$, in general. $DEL^{ij}(X^n)$ is the class that is formed by deleting, from each n-tuple of X^n, both its ith and j^{th} entries and then "closing it up" to form an $(n - 2)$-tuple. In general, $DEL^{ij}(Z^n) = Z^{n-2}$, and in particular $DEL^{12}(Z^2) = \perp$. If $X^2 \neq Z^2$, then $DEL^{12}(X^2) = \mathsf{T}$.

We may now define SD in terms of SEL and DEL as follows: If X^n is any class of n-tuples over D, and if $1 \leq i < j \leq n$, with $n \geq 2$, then

$$SD^{ij}(X^n) = DEL^{ij}[SEL^{ij}(X^n)] \quad .$$

We may note here that, if there is no n-tuple in X^n that contains the same member of D in both the ith and j^{th} places, then $SD^{ij}(X^n) = Z^{n-2}$ and, conversely, if $SD^{ij}(X^n) = Z^{n-2}$, then there is no n-tuple in X^n that contains the same member of D in both the ith and j^{th} places. Moreover, $SD^{ij}(Z^n) = Z^{n-2}$, in general, and in particular $SD^{12}(Z^2) = \perp$. If $X^2 \neq Z^2$ and X^2 contains at least one 2-tuple whose first and second entries are the same member of D, then $SD^{12}(X^2) = \mathsf{T}$; whereas, if X^2 contains no 2-tuple whose first and second entries are the same member of D, then $SD^{12}(X^2) = \perp$.

We may note here that $SEL^{12}(X^2)$ corresponds to what Peirce often called the "self part" of a dyadic relation viewed as a set of 2-tuples. It is also to be noted that $SD^{12}(X^2) = \bot$ if and only if $SEL^{12}(X^2) = Z^2$, that is if and only if the "self part" of X^2 is empty; and that $SD^{12}(X^2) = \top$ if and only if $SEL^{12}(X^2) \neq Z^2$, that is if and only if the "self part" of X^2 is not empty.

It is useful to introduce here generalizations of SEL and DEL, because these generalizations will be important later in this work. Let a class (matrix) of n-tuples X^n be given. And let the indices $i(1), i(2), \ldots, i(k)$ be given such that $1 \leq i(1) < i(2) < \ldots < i(k) \leq n$. Then we may define the generalized selection operation $SEL^{i(1)i(2)\cdots i(k)}$ by the equation

$$SEL^{i(1)i(2)\cdots i(k)}(X^n)$$

$$= SEL^{i(1)i(2)}\{\ldots SEL^{i(1)i(k-1)}[SEL^{i(1)i(k)}(X^n)]\ldots\} \quad .$$

$SEL^{i(1)i(2)\cdots i(k)}(X^n)$ is the class of all n-tuples of X^n that contain the same member of D in the $i(1)^{th}$, $i(2)^{th}$, $\ldots$, and $i(k)^{th}$ places; if no n-tuple of X^n has the same member of D in all these places, then $SEL^{i(1)i(2)\cdots i(k)}(X^n) = Z^n$. Clearly, $SEL^{i(1)i(2)\cdots i(k)}(Z^n) = Z^n$.

Now, let X^n be given as above, and let $1 \leq i \leq n$. Then we may define the singly-indexed Deletion operation DEL^i in this way. DEL^i is the class of all $(n - 1)$-tuples that is formed by first deleting, from each n-tuple of X^n, its ith entry and then "closing it up" to form an $(n - 1)$-tuple. (This is just Bernays's "Streichung" operation, perhaps preceded and followed by a permutation.) $DEL^i(Z^n) = Z^{n-1}$ in general, and in particular $DEL^1(Z^1) = \bot$. And, if $X^1 \neq Z^1$, then $Del^1(X^1) = \top$.

Now, with X^n given as above, let n and the indices $i(1), i(2), \ldots, i(k)$ be given such that $k \geq 1$ and $1 \leq i(1) < i(2) < \ldots < i(k) \leq n$. Then we may define the generalized deletion operation $DEL^{i(1)i(2)\cdots i(k)}$ by the equation

$$DEL^{i(1)i(2)\cdots i(k)}$$

$$= DEL^{i(1)}\{\ldots DEL^{i(k-1)}[DEL^{i(k)}(X^n)]\ldots\} \quad .$$

This is the class of all $(n - k)$-tuples formed by deleting from each n-tuple of X^n the $i(1)^{th}$, $i(2)^{th}$, $\ldots$, and $i(k)^{th}$ entries. $DEL^{i(1)i(2)\cdots i(k)}(Z^n) = Z^{n-k}$ in general, and in particular $DEL^{i(1)i(2)\cdots i(k)}(Z^k) = \bot$. And, if $X^k \neq Z^k$, then $DEL^{i(1)i(2)\cdots i(k)}(X^k) = \top$.

It may be noted that DEL^{ij}, as previously defined, is consistent with this account; that is,

$$DEL^{ij}(X^n) = DEL^i[DEL^j(X^n)] \quad .$$

With the four classes of operations thus defined, we may now proceed to define an *Enterpretation function* (or: *extensional valuation function*) *for PAL.* * is an Enterpretation function for PAL if it is a function from *terms of PAL* to *classes of n-tuples over some domain D and to finite sequences of classes of n-tuples over D* in the following way.

1. * assigns to each *primitive term* R_i^n of PAL a class of n-tuples over D, denoted by $*(R_i^n)$; furthermore, * operates as follows:

   $*(U^n) = V^n,$ for all $n \geq 1$;

   $*(0^n) = Z^n,$ for all $n \geq 1$;

   $*(1^n) = I^n,$ for all $n \geq 1$;

2. * assigns to each *element* E^n of adicity n of PAL a class of n- tuples over D, denoted by $*(E^n)$; furthermore, * operates in accord with the following conditions:

   $*[NEG(E^n)] = \langle *(E^n) \rangle$;

   $*[PERM_i^n(E^n)] = P_i^n[*(E^n)]$;

   $*[J_1^{ij}(E^n)] = SD^{ij}[*(E^n)]$; and

   $*[J_2^{ij}(E_1^n, E_2^m)] = SD^{ij}[*(E_1^n) \times *(E_2^m)]$.

3. * assigns to each *array* of elements of PAL, of adicity n, a finite sequence of classes of n-tuples over D, in such a way as to satisfy the condition that

   $*(E_1^{n_1} \circ E_2^{n_2} \circ \ldots \circ E_k^{n_k}) = *(E_1^{n_1}) \circ *(E_2^{n_2}) \circ \ldots \circ *(E_k^{n_k})$.

An *Enterpretation for PAL* is a pair consisting of a domain D and an Enterpretation function * mapping terms of PAL to classes, and to sequences of classes, of n-tuples over D. An Enterpretation may be indicated by writing the pair as (D,*).

Proposition 3.1: If $E_1, E_2, \ldots, E_k$ are any k elements of PAL; and if (D,*) and (D,\$) are two Enterpretations of PAL such that $*(E_i) = \$(E_i)$ for all i, $1 \leq i \leq k$, then

   $*(E_1 \circ E_2 \circ \ldots \circ E_k) = \$(E_1 \circ E_2 \circ \ldots \circ E_k)$.

Proof: By the definition of Enterpretation,

   $*(E_1 \circ E_2 \ldots \circ E_k) = *(E_1) \circ *(E_2) \circ \ldots \circ *(E_k)$.

By the hypothesis, the right-hand side of this equation is equal to

   $\$(E_1) \circ \$(E_2) \circ \ldots \circ \$(E_k)$.

By the definition of Enterpretation, this equals

$$\$(E_1 \circ E_2 \circ \ldots \circ E_k) \quad .$$

q.e.d.

Proposition 3.2: If E is an element of PAL; and if (D,*) and (D,$) are two Enterpretations of PAL on the same domain D such that for every primitive term $R_i^{n_i}$ of PAL occurring in E, $*(R_i^{n_i}) = \$(R_i^{n_i})$; then $*(E) = \$(E)$.

Proof: The proof is by induction on the length of an elementary derivation of E, together with the following facts:

(a) If E is any element of PAL such that $*(E) = \$(E)$, then $*[NEG(E)] = \$[NEG(E)]$;

(b) If E is any element of PAL such that $*(E) = \$(E)$, then $*[PERM_i^n(E)] = \$[PERM_i^n(E)]$;

(c) If E is any element of PAL such that $*(E) = \$(E)$, then $*[J_1^{ij}(E)] = \$[J_1^{ij}(E)]$;

(d) If E_1 and E_2 are any two elements of PAL such that $*(E_1) = \$(E_1)$ and $*(E_2) = \$(E_2)$, then $* [J_2^{ij}(E_1,E_2)] = \$ [J_2^{ij}(E_1,E_2)]$.

q.e.d.

Proposition 3.3: If $E_1, E_2, \ldots, E_k$ are any k elements of PAL; and if (D,*) and (D,$) are two Enterpretations of PAL on the same domain D such that, for every primitive term $R_i^{n_i}$ occurring in any of the E_i (with $1 \leq i \leq k$), we have that $*(R_i^{n_i}) = \$(R_i^{n_i})$; then:

$$*(E_1 \circ E_2 \circ \ldots \circ E_k) = \$(E_1 \circ E_2 \circ \ldots \circ E_k) \quad .$$

Proof: By Proposition 3.2, $*(E_i) = \$(E_i)$ for all i with $1 \leq i \leq k$. So, the result follows by applying Proposition 3.1.

q.e.d.

The exact notion of an Enterpretation for PAL allows us to define exactly the sense in which terms of PAL *depict, represent,* and *express.* These notions will be explicitly defined in connection with an arbitary array . Because, of course, all primitive terms of PAL are elements and all elements are being regarded as arrays of length 1, the definitions will be completely general.

Definition 3.3: Let any array α of PAL be given. Also, let an Enterpretation (D,*) for PAL be given. Then:

(1) α will be said *extensionally to depict, with regard to (D,*)* the *sequence* of classes of n-tuples $*(\alpha)$ over D;

(2) α will be said *extensionally to represent, with regard to (D, *)* the *class* of n-tuples $CP[*(\alpha)]$ over D; and

(3) α will be said *extensionally to express, with regard to (D, *)* the *class* of n-tuples $CP\{Ret[*(\alpha)]\}$ over D.

It is to be noted that, although the concepts of depiction, representation, and expression differ from one another, it is nevertheless the case that, for any array, the adicity of the sequence of classes of n-tuples depicted is the same number as the adicity of the class of n-tuples represented and the adicity of the class of n-tuples expressed. It is also to be noted that if α has *only* elements of adicity 0 occurring in it as entries, then $CP\{Ret[*(\alpha)]\} = CP\{CP[*(\alpha)]\} = CP[*(\alpha)]$; so that, for such arrays, representation and expression come to the same thing. It is also to be noted that if α has *no* elements of adicity 0 occurring in it as entries, then $Ret[*(\alpha)] = *(\alpha)$, so that $CP\{Ret[*(\alpha)]\} = CP[*(\alpha)]$; so that for such arrays also, representation and expression come to the same thing. Representation and expression differ only with regard to arrays that have at least one entry of adicity 0 *and* at least one entry of adicity $n \geq 1$.

With the notion of an Enterpretation function and thus the notion of an Enterpretation, we may now define *truth* for a primitive well-formed formula of PAL

$$t_1 = t_2 \quad .$$

We first define truth for such a formula with respect to an Enterpretation (D,*). The formula $t_1 = t_2$ is true with respect to the Enterpretation (D,*) if and only if

$$CP[*(t_1)] = CP[*(t_2)] \quad .$$

That is to say, the formula $t_1 = t_2$ is true with respect to the Enterpretation (D,*) if and only if the two terms *represent*, with regard to (D,*), the same class of n-tuples over D.

We may now define *extensional logical truth* for primitive formulae of PAL. A primitive formula of PAL is *logically true* in the extensional sense if and only if it is true with respect to *every* Enterpretation (D,*).

If $t_1 = t_2$ is logically true in the extensional sense, then t_1 may be said to be *logically equivalent to* t_2.

4

SEMANTICS FOR PEIRCEAN ALGEBRAIC LOGIC, PART TWO

The purport of PAL is to be a logic whose terms stand for relations, relations *as such* and not merely sets or even "classes of n-tuples." The Enterpretations of the preceding section do not fully capture this idea. In order to capture it, a concept of a "relation *simpliciter*" is obviously needed. Such a concept must, however, be removed from the realm of the psychological in order to make it precise enough for standard logical purposes. Before developing the formalism by which the present section of this work seeks to capture the notion of a "relation *simpliciter*," and thereby a genuinely-though-still-precisely *intensional* notion of an Interpretation of the terms of PAL, some informal and "motivational" discussion is useful.

Let us begin with the informal concept of a "possible world," and with the informal concept of "the collection W of all possible worlds." These concepts—though they have many philosophical detractors—have animated and fueled most of the progress in modal logic since the publication of Kripke's groundbreaking paper "A Completeness Theorem in Modal Logic" (Kripke, 1959). Each possible world w in W has its domain D_w, which may be conceived as the set of all entities existent in w. Now, an n-adic predicate together with an understanding of its "meaning," may be regarded as picking out, for every possible world w, precisely those n-tuples over D_w that "satisfy" it. In effect, therefore, an n-adic relation may be identified with a specification for each and every possible world of a collection of n-tuples over that world's domain.

A standing problem with possible-world semantics for modal logic is to make precise sense of the notion of a possible world. The present intensional semantics for PAL avoids addressing this problem. In it, the functional role played in modal semantics by the notion of a possible world is played instead by the notion of a *domain*, as given in the previous section; the functional role played in modal semantics by the collection W of all possible worlds is played instead by the notion of a *set W* that intuitively is understood to index *all domains*. This work's reference to possible worlds is to be understood as heuristic only. The semantics is meant to stand on its own, quite aside from the informal possible-worlds picture. The semantics herein developed, the notion of an Interpretation, and the resultant defined notions of this section need to presuppose only the notion of sets and nothing more exotic.

Let us define a *model structure* M = (W, D) for PAL to be a set W of indices, and a set D of non-empty sets D_w indexed by W, such that for each w of W the indexed set D_w of D contains neither the truth value $\top$ nor the truth value $\bot$. Each D_w will be called the *domain* of its index w. Obviously, each domain of an index w in W is a domain in the sense of the previous section of this work. The crucial concept to be introduced in defining the notion of an Interpretation for PAL is the concept of a *relation-simpliciter.*

Definition 4.1: For each D_w in D, let C_w be the set of all classes of n-tuples, for n = 0,1,2, . . . , over D_w (in the sense of the preceding section of this work). And let C be the set of all such C_w, for w in W. Then, a *relation-simpliciter of adicity n* is, by definition, a function ψ from W to $\cup C$ such that for each w of W, $\psi(w)$ is a class of n-tuples X^n over D_w (in the sense of the preceding section of this work); equivalently, $\psi(w)$ is a class of n-tuples X^n in C_w.

Intuitively, this definition means that a relation-simpliciter is a once-for-all specification, for each possible world, of the *extension* of that relation-simpliciter with respect to that world. The 0-adic relation-simpliciter TRUE, or $UNIV^0$, is the relation-simpliciter taking every w in W to the truth value $\top$. The 0-adic relation-simpliciter FALSE, or $NULL^0$, is the relation-simpliciter taking every w in W to the truth value $\bot$. For $n \geq 1$, the n-adic relation-simpliciter $UNIV^n$ is the relation-simpliciter taking every w in W to the universal class $(V^n)_w$ of n-tuples over D_w. For $n \geq 1$, the n-adic relation-simpliciter $NULL^n$ is the relation-simpliciter taking every w in W to the null class $(Z^n)_w$ of n-tuples over D_w. For $n \geq 2$, the n-adic relation-simpliciter ID^n is the relation-simpliciter taking every w in W to the identity class $(I^n)_w$ of n-tuples over D_w.

Finite sequences of relations-simpliciter will be written with the same symbol, namely °, that is used to write arrays of PAL and finite sequences of classes of n-tuples. As with arrays of PAL and with finite sequences of classes of n-tuples over a domain, a sequence of relations-simpliciter of length 1, and a single relation-simpliciter, will be regarded as simply being the same thing.

The adicity of a sequence of relations-simpliciter is simply the sum of the adicities of all its entries.

To any finite sequence of relations-simpliciter $\psi_1 \circ \psi_2 \circ \ldots \circ \psi_k$, there corresponds a function ψ from W to the set of finite sequences of members of $\cup C$, where ψ is defined such that, for all w of W,

$$\psi(w) = \psi_1(w) \circ \psi_2(w) \circ \ldots \circ \psi_k(w) \quad .$$

As the name of this corresponding function, we will use the sequence itself of relations-simpliciter to which it corresponds. In this manner, we may write in general that

$$[\psi_1 \circ \psi_2 \circ \ldots \circ \psi_k](w) = \psi_1(w) \circ \psi_2(w) \circ \ldots \circ \psi_k(w) \quad .$$

The notion of retracting a sequence of relations-simpliciter duplicates the notion of retracting a sequence of classes of n-tuples. In order to define retraction exactly, the Cartesian Product operator first must be introduced in the intensional context.

We may now define in the intensional context the operations of complementation, permutations, Cartesian Product, selective double deletion, the selection operations, and the deletion operations as applied to relations-simpliciter. In the following definitions, it is, of course, assumed as given that all subscripts, superscripts, and arguments are "consistent with adicity."

The complement relation-simpliciter $\langle \Re \rangle$ of a relation-simpliciter $\Re$ is defined as the relation-simpliciter such that, for all w of W, $\langle \Re \rangle(\omega) = \langle \Re(w) \rangle$.

The permutation relation-simpliciter $P_i^n(\Re)$ of a relation-simpliciter $\Re$ is defined as the relation-simpliciter such that, for all w of W, $[P_i^n(\Re)](w) = P_i^n[\Re(w)]$.

The Cartesian Product relation-simpliciter $\Re_1 \times \Re_2 \times \ldots \times \Re_j$ of relations-simpliciter $\Re_1, \Re_2, \ldots, \Re_j$, in that order, is the relation-simpliciter such that, for all w of W,

$$[\Re_1 \times \Re_2 \times \ldots \times \Re_j](w) = \Re_1(w) \times \Re_2(w) \times \ldots \times \Re_j(w) \quad .$$

We may note here that for any relation-simpliciter $\Re$ of *any* adicity k, $NULL^n \times \Re = \Re \times NULL^n = NULL^{n+k}$. We may also note that if $\Re$ is *any* relation-simpliciter of *any* adicity n, then $TRUE \times \Re = \Re \times TRUE = \Re$, and that $FALSE \times \Re = \Re \times FALSE = NULL^n$. In particular, $TRUE \times TRUE = TRUE$, and $TRUE \times FALSE = FALSE \times TRUE = FALSE \times FALSE = FALSE$.

We may now define the intensional Cartesian Product operator CP, which is an operator on finite sequences of relations-simpliciter, as follows. Let $\sigma = \Re_1 \circ \Re_2 \circ \ldots \circ \Re_k$ be such a sequence. Then $CP(\sigma)$ is the Cartesian Product relation-simpliciter

$$\Re_1 \times \Re_2 \times \ldots \times \Re_k \quad .$$

As with the extensional Cartesian Product operator, the intensional Cartesian Product operator CP simply replaces each occurrence of the symbol $\circ$ in a sequence with the operator for Cartesian Product. (Also, as with the extensional Cartesian Product operator, if σ is a sequence of length 1, that is, is a single relation-simpliciter, then $CP(\sigma) = \sigma$.) The notion of retraction in the intensional context duplicates the notion of retraction in the extensional context, and we may define an intensional retraction operator Ret on such sequences.

Definition 4.2: Let σ be any finite sequence of relations-simpliciter. Then we define *the retraction of* σ, $\text{Ret}(\sigma)$, as follows:

(1) If σ has *no* relations-simpliciter of adicity 0 occurring as entries in it, then $\text{Ret}(\sigma) = \sigma$;

(2) If σ has *only* relations-simpliciter of adicity 0 occurring as entries in it, then $\text{Ret}(\sigma) = CP(\sigma)$;

(3) If σ has at least one entry that is a relation-simpliciter of adicity 0 *and* at least one entry that is a relation-simpliciter of adicity n, with $n \geq 1$, then $\text{Ret}(\sigma)$ is the sequence of relations-simpliciter obtained from σ by extracting from it all entries that are relations-simpliciter of adicity 0 and then shortening its length accordingly.

The ijth selective double deletion relation-simpliciter $SD^{ij}(\Re)$ of a relation-simpliciter $\Re$, also written as $SD^{i,j}(\Re)$, is defined as the relation-simpliciter such that, for all w of W, $[SD^{ij}(\Re)](w) = SD^{ij}[\Re(w)]$.

The generalized intensional selection operations $SEL^{i(1)i(2)\cdots i(k)}$ and the generalized intensional deletion operations $DEL^{i(1)i(2)\cdots i(k)}$ are similarly defined: namely so that, for all w of W,

$$[SEL^{i(1)i(2)\cdots i(k)}(\Re)](w) = SEL^{i(1)i(2)\cdots i(k)}[\Re(w)] \quad,$$

and

$$[DEL^{i(1)i(2)\cdots i(k)}(\Re)](w) = DEL^{i(1)i(2)\cdots i(k)}[\Re(w)] \quad.$$

It should be noticed that the symbols being used to designate the operations of the intensional semantics for PAL are the same symbols as those used to designate the operations of the extensional semantics for PAL. The advantage of using the operation symbols to do double-duty in this way is that doing so facilitates greatly the task of presenting the connections between the extensional semantics and the intensional semantics. The minor disadvantage, namely that one may not instantly know whether an operation symbol is being used in an intensional or extensional manner, can be easily overcome simply by looking at the arguments of the operations.

Given the understanding of a relation-simpliciter, as just discussed, we are now ready for the definition of an Interpretation of PAL. To this end we first define the concept of an *intensional valuation function*. An *intensional valuation function* ι *for PAL* is a function taking terms of PAL to relations-simpliciter and to finite sequences of relations-simpliciter, such that, if E^n is an element of PAL of adicity n, then $\iota(E^n)$ is a relation-simpliciter of adicity n, and if t^n is an array $E_1 \circ E_2 \circ \ldots \circ E_k$ of elements of PAL, then $\iota(t^n)$ is the finite sequence of relations-simpliciter

$$\iota(E_1) \circ \iota(E_2) \circ \ldots \circ \iota(E_k) \quad .$$

Now, an *Interpretation* of PAL is a special kind of intensional valuation function for PAL. In order to understand exactly what kind, we must take note that every intensional valuation function induces, for each w of W, a function from terms of PAL to classes of n-tuples over D_w and sequences of classes of n-tuples over D_w in a certain way, namely in such a way as to make this induced function a candidate for an Enterpretation function. Let us be more precise about this matter.

First, notice that if ι is an intensional valuation function for PAL, then for any element E^n of adicity n of PAL, $\iota(E^n)$ is a relation-simpliciter of adicity n. So, if w is any member of W, then $[\iota(E^n)](w)$ is a class X^n of n-tuples over D_w. Thus, any intensional valuation function ι for PAL induces, for each w of W, a function $**_{\iota w}$ from elements of PAL to classes of n-tuples over D_w, namely the function $**_{\iota w}$ defined by

$$**_{\iota w}(E^n) = [\iota(E^n)](w) \quad ,$$

for all elements E^n of PAL.

Second, notice that if ι is an intensional valuation function for PAL, then for any array $E_1 \circ E_2 \circ \ldots \circ E_k$ of PAL, $\iota(E_1 \circ E_2 \circ \ldots \circ E_k)$ is the finite sequence of relations-simpliciter

$$\iota(E_1) \circ \iota(E_2) \circ \ldots \circ \iota(E_k) \quad .$$

Thus, any intensional valuation function ι induces, for each w of W, a function $*_{\iota w}$ from arrays of PAL to finite sequences of classes of n-tuples over D_w, namely the function $*_{\iota w}$ defined by

$$*_{tw}(E_1 \circ E_2 \circ \ldots \circ E_k) = [\iota(E_1 \circ E_2 \circ \ldots \circ E_k)](w)$$
$$= [\iota(E_1) \circ \iota(E_2) \circ \ldots \circ \iota(E_k)](w)$$
$$= [\iota(E_1)](w) \circ [\iota(E_2)](w) \circ \ldots \circ [\iota(E_k)](w)$$
$$= **_{tw}(E_1) \circ **_{tw}(E_2) \circ \ldots \circ **_{tw}(E_k) \quad .$$

The function $*_{tw}$ coincides, of course, with the function $**_{tw}$ on arrays of chorisis 1, that is, on elements. So $*_{tw}$ is a function from terms of PAL to classes of n-tuples over D_w and sequences of classes of n-tuples over D_w in the manner of an Enterpretation function. This point is prefatory to the following definion.

Definition 4.3: By definition, ι is an *Interpretation for PAL* if and only if ι is an intensional valuation function for PAL such that *for every w in W* the function $*_{tw}$ induced by ι is an *Enterpretation function* for PAL, so that the pair $(D_w, *_{tw})$ is an *Enterpretation* for PAL in the sense of the previous section of this work.

Truth of primitive formulae of PAL with respect to the intensionalist semantics for PAL is defined in a manner analogous to the manner in which truth of primitive formulae was defined with respect to the extensionalist semantics for PAL. The formula $t_1 = t_2$ is true with respect to the Interpretation ι if and only if

$$CP[\iota(t_1)] = CP[\iota(t_2)] \quad .$$

A formula is *logically true in the intensional sense* if and only if it is true with respect to *every* Interpretation . If a formula is logically true in the extensionalist sense, then it is logically true in the intensionalist sense.

The following theorem explicates the interaction between Interpretation functions and the operations involved in the semantics for PAL. It should be compared with the definition of an Enterpretation function in the previous section.

Theorem 4.1: Let ι be any Interpretation for PAL. Then the following obtain (where it is understood that all subscripts and superscripts are "consistent with adicity," as previously defined):

(1) ι assigns to each *primitive term* R_i^n of PAL a relation-simpliciter of adicity n, denoted by $\iota(R_i^n)$; furthermore, ι operates as follows:

$\iota(U^n) = UNIV^n$, for all $n \geq 1$;

$\iota(0^n) = NULL^n$, for all $n \geq 1$;

$\iota(1^n) = ID^n$, for all $n \geq 2$.

(2) ι assigns to each *element* E^n of adicity n of PAL a relation-simpliciter of adicity n, denoted by $\iota(E^n)$; furthermore, ι operates in accord with the following conditions:

$\iota[NEG(E^n)] = \langle\iota(E^n)\rangle$;

$\iota[PERM_i^n(E^n)] = P_i^n[\iota(E^n)]$;

$\iota[J_1^{ij}(E^n)] = SD^{ij}[\iota(E^n)]$;

$\iota[J_2^{ij}(E_1^n, E_2^m)] = SD^{ij}[\iota(E_1^n) \times \iota(E_2^m)]$.

(3) ι assigns to each *array* of elements of PAL, of adicity n, a sequence of adicity n of relations-simpliciter; furthermore, ι operates in such a way as to satisfy the condition that

$\iota(E_1^{n_1} \circ E_2^{n_2} \circ \ldots \circ E_k^{n_k}) = \iota(E_1^{n_1}) \circ \iota(E_2^{n_2}) \circ \ldots \circ \iota(E_k^{n_k})$.

Proof: The proof of (1) and (2) is straightforward and will be omitted. Clause (3) is simply part of the definition of an Interpretation.

q.e.d.

The connections between the Enterpretations $(D,*)$ of the previous section of this work and the Interpretations ι of the present section are straightforward and systematic. Each Interpretation ι induces a family of Enterpretations $(D_w, *_{\iota w})$, one such for each w of W. It therefore follows that if a result can be proved for *all* Enterpretations $(D,*)$, then this result applies to all Enterpretations $(D_w, *_{\iota w})$ induced by all Interpretations ι. Thus, as Theorem 4.1 illustrates, there is an intimate structural connection between the extensional semantics of the previous section and the intensional semantics of the present section: we have, in fact, a structural identity. This means that results from the analysis of the extensional semantics for PAL can simply be carried over, with minor differences (and of course with care), to results about the intensional semantics for PAL. We see three examples of such carrying over in the following Corollaries to Theorem 4.1. The first is the intensional analogue of Proposition 3.1.

Corollary 4.1.1: If E_1, E_2, . . . ,E_k are any k elements of PAL; and if ι and γ are two Interpretations of PAL such that $\iota(E_i) = \gamma(E_i)$ for all i, $1 \leq i \leq k$, then

$\iota(E_1 \circ E_2 \circ \ldots \circ E_k) = \gamma(E_1 \circ E_2 \circ \ldots \circ E_k)$.

Proof: The proof is obtained simply by writing out the intensional analogue of the proof for Proposition 3.1.

The next Corollary is the intensional analogue of Proposition 3.2.

Corollary 4.1.2: If E is an element of PAL; and if ι and γ are any two Interpretations for PAL such that, for every primitive term $R_i^{n_i}$ of PAL occurring in E, $\iota(R_i^{n_i}) = \gamma(R_i^{n_i})$; then

$$\iota(E) = \gamma(E) \quad .$$

Proof: The proof is by induction on the length of an elementary derivation of E, together with the following facts:

(a) If E is any element of PAL such that $\iota(E) = \gamma(E)$, then $\iota[NEG(E)] = \gamma[NEG(E)]$.

(b) If E is any element of PAL such that $\iota(E) = \gamma(E)$, then $\iota[PERM_i^n(E)] = \gamma[PERM_i^n(E)]$.

(c) If E is any element of PAL such that $\iota(E) = \gamma(E)$, then $\iota[J_1^{ij}(E)] = \gamma[J_1^{ij}(E)]$.

(d) If E_1 and E_2 are any two elements of PAL such that $\iota(E_1) = \gamma(E_1)$ and $\iota(E_2) = \gamma(E_2)$, then $\iota[J_2^{ij}(E_1,E_2)] = \gamma[J_2^{ij}(E_1,E_2)]$.

The proofs of facts (a)-(d) are straightforward and will thus be omitted.

q.e.d.

The next Corollary is the intensional analogue of Proposition 3.3.

Corollary 4.1.3: If E_1, E_2, . . . , E_k are any k elements of PAL; and if ι and γ are two Interpretations for PAL such that, for every primitive term $R_i^{n_i}$ occurring in any of the E_i (with $1 \leq i \leq k$), we have that $\iota(R_i^{n_i}) = \gamma(R_i^{n_i})$; then

$$\iota(E_1 \circ E_2 \circ \ldots \circ E_k) = \gamma(E_1 \circ E_2 \circ \ldots \circ E_k) \quad .$$

Proof: By Corollary 4.1.2, $\iota(E_i) = \gamma(E_i)$ for all i with $1 \leq i \leq k$. So the result follows from applying Corollary 4.1.1.

q.e.d.

We are now in a position to define several very important properties of relations-simpliciter.

Definition 4.4: A relation-simpliciter $\Re$ of adicity k will be said to be *composite* if and only if there are two integers $n \geq 1$, $m \geq 1$, such that $n + m = k$ and such that for *every* w of W, $\Re(w)$ is a Cartesian Product $X_w^n \times Y_w^m$ of a class of n-tuples X_w^n over D_w and a class of m-tuples Y_w^m over D_w.

The following propositions are immediate:

Proposition 4.1: If a relation-simpliciter $\Re$ of adicity k is composite, then $k \geq 2$.

Proposition 4.2: A relation-simpliciter $\Re$ of adicity k is composite if and only if there are j integers (with $2 \leq j \leq k$) $n_1, n_2, \ldots, n_j$, with each $n_i \geq 1$ and with $n_1 + n_2 + \ldots + n_j = k$, such that for every w of W, $\Re(w)$ is a Cartesian Product

$$X_{1w}^{n_1} \times X_{2w}^{n_2} \times \ldots \times X_{jw}^{n_j}$$

of j classes of tuples $X_{1w}^{n_1}, X_{2w}^{n_2}, \ldots, X_{jw}^{n_j}$, with each $X_{iw}^{n_i}$ being a class of n_i-tuples over D_w.

Proof: The proof follows immediately from the associativity of Cartesian Product and the fact that a Cartesian Product of more than 2 factors can always be represented as a Cartesian product of exactly two factors, for example its first factor and the Cartesian Product of all its remaining factors.

q.e.d.

Proposition 4.3: A relation-simpliciter $\Re$ of adicity k is composite if and only if there are j integers (with $2 \leq j \leq k$) $n_1, n_2, \ldots, n_j$, with each $n_i \geq 1$ and with $n_1 + n_2 + \ldots + n_j = k$; *and* there are j relations-simpliciter $\Re_1, \Re_2, \ldots, \Re_j$, of adicities $n_1, n_2, \ldots, n_j$, respectively, such that

$$\Re = \Re_1 \times \Re_2 \times \ldots \times \Re_j \quad .$$

Proof: (IF) Assume that $\Re$ is the indicated Cartesian Product of j relations-simpliciter. Then, for every w of W, $\Re(w) = [\Re_1 \times \Re_2 \times \ldots \times \Re_j](w)$, which by definition of Cartesian Product is equivalent to

$$[\Re_1](w) \times [\Re_2](w) \times \ldots \times [\Re_j](w) \quad .$$

But now each $[\Re_i](w)$ is a class of n_i-tuples over D_w. Thus, by Proposition 4.2, $\Re$ is composite.

(ONLY IF) Assume that $\Re$ is composite, so that the specification of Proposition 4.2 applies to $\Re$. Then, for each i with $1 \leq i \leq j$, let $\Re_i$ be the relation-simpliciter such that, for every w of W,

$$[\Re_i](w) = X_{iw}^{n_i} \quad .$$

Then, $\Re = \Re_1 \times \Re_2 \times \ldots \times \Re_j$.

q.e.d.

Definition 4.5: A relation-simpliciter $\Re$ of adicity k is, by definition, *degenerate* if and only if there are j integers (with $2 \leq j \leq k$) $n_1, n_2, \ldots, n_j$, with each n_i such that $1 \leq n_i \leq 2$ and with $n_1 + n_2 + \ldots + n_j = k$, such that for every w of W, $\Re(w)$ is a Cartesian Product

$$X_{1w}^{n_1} \times X_{2w}^{n_2} \times \ldots \times X_{jw}^{n_j}$$

of j classes of tuples $X_{1w}{}^{n_1}$, $X_{2w}{}^{n_2}$, . . . , $X_{jw}{}^{n_j}$, with each $X_{iw}{}^{n_i}$ being a class of n_i-tuples over D_w.

Proposition 4.4: A relation-simpliciter is degenerate only if it is composite.

Proof: Obvious.

Proposition 4.5: If a relation-simpliciter $\Re$ of adicity k is degenerate, then $k \geq 2$.

Proof: Obvious from Proposition 4.1 and Proposition 4.4.

Proposition 4.6: A relation-simpliciter $\Re$ of adicity k is degenerate if and only if there are j integers (with $2 \leq j \leq k$) $n_1, n_2, \ldots, n_j$, with each n_i such that $1 \leq n_i \leq 2$, and with $n_1 + n_2 + \ldots + n_j = k$; *and* there are j relations-simpliciter $\Re_1, \Re_2, \ldots, \Re_j$, of adicities $n_1, n_2, \ldots, n_j$, respectively; such that

$$\Re = \Re_1 \times \Re_2 \times \ldots \times \Re_j \quad .$$

Proof: This proposition parallels Proposition 4.3 regarding compositeness, except that where Proposition 4.3 contains the condition $n_i \geq 1$, this proposition contains the condition $1 \leq n_i \leq 2$. Hence, the proof of this proposition runs exactly like the proof of Proposition 4.3.

q.e.d

From this point on in this work, instead of continuing to write "relation-simpliciter" to designate relations-simpliciter, we will write simply "relation."

We now begin to explicate precisely and in full concepts that were only partially introduced earlier, the concepts, namely, of what it is for terms of PAL to *depict*, to *represent*, and to *express* relations.

Definition 4.6: Let any array α of PAL be given. (Because elements are being regarded as arrays of chorisis or length 1, the definitions will be completely general.) And let any Interpretation ι for PAL be given. Then:

(1) α will be said to *depict on* ι the *sequence of relations* $\iota(\alpha)$;

(2) α will be said to *represent on* ι the *relation* $CP[\iota(\alpha)]$; and

(3) α will be said to *express on* ι the *relation* $CP\{Ret[\iota(\alpha)]\}$.

By definition also, a term t (that is, an array) of PAL will be said to *denote* a relation $\Re$ if and only if t expresses $\Re$ on *every* interpretation ι. Also by definition, a relation $\Re$ is *expressible* by a term t of PAL if and only if there is *some* Interpretation ι such that $CP\{Ret[\iota(t)]\} = \Re$. In other words, $\Re$ is expressible by t if and only if there is some interpretation ι such that t expresses $\Re$ on ι. If a relation $\Re$ is of adicity k_1, then $\Re$ is expressible by a term t of PAL of adicity k_2 only if $k_1 = k_2$; also, if t is a *primitive term* other than one of the *constant* primitive terms, then $k_1 = k_2 \geq 1$ *suffices* for $\mathfrak{R}$'s being expressible by t. For, let ι be any Interpretation such that $\iota(t) = \mathfrak{R}$. Because $\mathfrak{R}$ is a single relation, $\text{Ret}(\mathfrak{R}) = \mathfrak{R}$, and thus $\text{CP}\{\text{Ret}[\iota(t)]\} = \mathfrak{R}$.

As in the extensional context, it is to be noted that, although the concepts of depiction, representation, and expression differ from one another, it is nevertheless the case that, for any array, the adicity of the sequence of relations depicted is the same number as the adicity of the relation represented and the adicity of the relation expressed. It is also to be noted that if an array α has *only* elements of adicity 0 occurring in it as entries, then $\text{CP}\{\text{Ret}[\iota(\alpha)]\} = \text{CP}\{\text{CP}\{[\iota(\alpha)]\} = \text{CP}[\iota(\alpha)]$; so that, for such arrays, representation and expression come to the same thing. It is also to be noted that, if α has *no* elements of adicity 0 occurring in it as entries, then $\text{Ret}[\iota(\alpha)] = \iota(\alpha)$, so that $\text{CP}\{\text{Ret}[\iota(\alpha)]\} = \text{CP}[\iota(\alpha)]$; so that for such arrays also, representation and expression come to the same thing. Representation and expression differ only with regard to arrays that have at least one entry of adicity 0 *and* at least one entry of adicity $n \geq 1$. For example, let E^0 be an element of adicity 0 that denotes the relation FALSE. Then $E^0 \circ U^n$ *represents*, on any Interpretation, the relation NULL^n; but it *expresses*, on any Interpretation, the relation UNIV^n. If an array α is a single element (that is, is an array of chorisis 1), and if ι is an Interpretation, then the relation depicted, represented, and expressed on ι by α is the same, namely $\iota(\alpha)$.

Several Propositions concerning the just-defined notions are now in order.

Proposition 4.7: The term U^n of PAL denotes the universal relation UNIV^n, for all $n \geq 1$.

The term 0^n of PAL denotes the null relation NULL^n, for all $n \geq 1$.

The term 1^n of PAL denotes the identity relation ID^n, for all $n \geq 2$.

Proposition 4.8: If a term t^n of PAL, of adicity n, is an array of elements of PAL of size ≥ 2, then t^n expresses a composite relation on *every* Interpretation.

Proof: Let a term t^n of PAL be an array of size ≥ 2; and let any Interpretation ι be given. Then

$$\iota(t^n) = \mathfrak{R}_1{}^{n_1} \circ \mathfrak{R}_2{}^{n_2} \circ \ldots \circ \mathfrak{R}_j{}^{n_j} \quad ,$$

where at least two of the n_i are ≥ 1. Consequently,

$$\text{Ret}[\iota(t^n)] = \mathfrak{R}_{i(1)}{}^{n_{i(1)}} \circ \mathfrak{R}_{i(2)}{}^{n_{i(2)}} \circ \ldots \circ \mathfrak{R}_{i(k)}{}^{n_{i(k)}} \quad ,$$

where each superscript $n_{i(m)}$ is ≥ 1 and where $k \geq 2$. It follows that

$$CP\{Ret[\iota(t^n)]\} = \mathfrak{R}_{i(1)}{}^{n_{i(1)}} \times \mathfrak{R}_{i(2)}{}^{n_{i(2)}} \times \ldots \times \mathfrak{R}_{i(k)}{}^{n_{i(k)}} \quad ,$$

which, by Proposition 4.3, is a composite relation. Hence, t^n expresses a composite relation on ι.

q.e.d.

Proposition 4.9: If a term t^n of PAL, of adicity n, is an array of elements of PAL of size ≥ 2, *and* if every element occurring in the array t^n is of adicity ≤ 2, then t^n expresses a degenerate relation on *every* Interpretation.

Proof: The proof duplicates that of the proof of Proposition 4.8, except that in place of citing Proposition 4.3, the proof cites Proposition 4.6.

Proposition 4.10: If a relation $\mathfrak{R}$ of adicity k is composite, then it is expressible by a term t^n of PAL that is an array of PAL of size ≥ 2.

Proof: For, given a composite relation $\mathfrak{R}$ of adicity k, let $\mathfrak{R}_1, \mathfrak{R}_2, \ldots, \mathfrak{R}_j$, and $n_1, n_2, \ldots, n_j$ be as in Proposition 4.3, so that

$$\mathfrak{R} = \mathfrak{R}_1 \times \mathfrak{R}_2 \times \ldots \times \mathfrak{R}_j \quad .$$

And let any j primitive terms $R_1{}^{n_1}, R_2{}^{n_2}, \ldots, R_j{}^{n_j}$ of PAL, of adicities $n_1, n_2, \ldots, n_j$, respectively, be given. Now, an Interpretation ι may be defined such that for all i, with $1 \leq i \leq j$, $\iota(R_i{}^{n_i}) = \mathfrak{R}_i$. (On the other primitive terms of PAL ι may be defined as one pleases.) Then the array

$$\alpha = R_1{}^{n_1} \circ R_2{}^{n_2} \circ \ldots \circ R_j{}^{n_j}$$

is of adicity k and size ≥ 2. Furthermore,

$$\iota(\alpha) = \iota(R_1{}^{n_1} \circ R_2{}^{n_2} \circ \ldots \circ R_j{}^{n_j})$$
$$= \iota(R_1{}^{n_1}) \circ \iota(R_2{}^{n_2}) \circ \ldots \circ \iota(R_j{}^{n_j})$$
$$= \mathfrak{R}_1 \circ \mathfrak{R}_2 \circ \ldots \circ \mathfrak{R}_j \quad .$$

Now, because each $n_i \geq 1$, $Ret[\iota(\alpha)] = \iota(\alpha)$, so that $CP\{Ret[\iota(\alpha)]\} = CP[\iota(\alpha)] = \mathfrak{R}_1 \times \mathfrak{R}_2 \times \ldots \times \mathfrak{R}_j = \mathfrak{R}$. Thus, α expresses on ι the relation $\mathfrak{R}$.

q.e.d.

Proposition 4.11: If a relation $\mathfrak{R}$ of adicity k is degenerate, then it is expressible by a term t^n of PAL that is an array of PAL of size ≥ 2 and furthermore is such that each occurrence of an element of PAL in it is of *adicity 1* or *adicity 2* and hence is of adicity ≤ 2.

Proof: The proof is exactly like the proof of Proposition 4.10.

Theorem 4.2: A relation $\mathfrak{R}$ of adicity k is composite if and only if it is expressible by an array of PAL of size ≥ 2.

Proof: By Proposition 4.8 and Proposition 4.10.

Theorem 4.3: A relation $\mathfrak{R}$ of adicity k is degenerate if and only if it is expressible by an array of PAL of size ≥ 2 and furthermore such that each occurrence of an element in the array is of adicity ≤ 2.

Proof: By Proposition 4.9 and Proposition 4.11.

Proposition 4.12: A relation $\mathfrak{R}$ of adicity k is composite if and only if there are positive integers $n_1, n_2, \ldots, n_j$ with $n_1 + n_2 + \ldots + n_j = k$, and there are primitive terms of PAL, $R_1{}^{n_1}, R_2{}^{n_2}, \ldots, R_j{}^{n_j}$, such that $\mathfrak{R}$ is expressible in the form

$$R_1{}^{n_1} \circ R_2{}^{n_2} \circ \ldots \circ R_j{}^{n_j} \quad .$$

Proposition 4.13: A relation $\mathfrak{R}$ is degenerate if and only if the above conditions for compositeness are met and furthermore each n_i is no greater than 2 (so that for all n_i, $1 \leq n_i \leq 2$).

It is thus clear that a dyadic relation is degenerate if and only if it may be expressed in the form $P^1 \circ Q^1$; it is also clear that a triadic relation is degenerate if and only if it may be expressed in one of the three forms: (a) $P^1 \circ Q^1 \circ N^1$; or (b) $P^1 \circ R^2$; or (c) $R^2 \circ P^1$. We may note here that for $n \geq 2$, the universal relations $UNIV^n$ and the null relations $NULL^n$ are degenerate.

NOTES

1. In order to be a bit more exact, let us note that model structures may vary from one to the other. This fact means that the various definitions of intensional concepts that are introduced in this work must be understood to incorporate implicit reference to some particular model structure. At the extreme lower limit, of course, the model structure might consist of a set of indices W containing just one member, so that with respect to such a structure the difference between intensional and extensional semantics would collapse. In general, however, the difference will not collapse. For the sake of clarity of exposition, the practice has been adopted in this work of making explicit reference to the background model structure only when a particular result depends on doing so.

5

DEGENERACY AND THE CONSTRUCTIBILITY
OF RELATIONS

In this section, another of the crucial notions involved in the reduction thesis of this work is defined. Then the main negative reduction results are proved.

The crucial notion for understanding the reduction thesis is the notion of the *constructibility* of terms of PAL and of relations (that is, of course, relations-*simpliciter*). The notion of the constructibility of *relations* is defined by means of the notion of the constructibility of *terms* of PAL.

Let there be given an arbitrary assembly $A = [E_1, E_2, \ldots, E_k]$ consisting of elements from some set ξ of elements. We define an *immediate derivative* A' of A to be any assembly A' such that one of the six following statements obtains about how A is related to A':

(1) $A' = A$;

(2) A' is of the same chorisis as A and differs from A only in respect of one occurrence of an element: namely, where A has an occurrence of an element E_i, A' has an occurrence of the element $NEG(E_i)$;

(3) A' is of the same chorisis as A and differs from A only in respect of one occurrence of an element: namely, where A has an occurrence of an element E_i, A' has an occurrence of the element $PERM_j^n(E_i)$, (where j, n are restricted so and only so as to be consistent with the definition of PERM);

(4) A' is of the same chorisis as A and differs from A only in respect of one occurrence of an element: namely, where A has an occurrence of an element E_i, A' has an occurrence of the element $J_1^{pq}(E_i)$, (where p,q, and the adicity of E_i are restricted so and only so as to be consistent with the definition of $Join_1$;

(5) A' is of chorisis *less by 1* than the chorisis of A, and A' differs from A only in respect of *both lacking* two occurrences of elements of A (namely, an occurrence of an element E_i and an occurrence of an element E_j (perhaps occurrences of the same element), *and containing* an additional occurrence: namely, an occurrence of the element $J_2^{pq}(E_i,E_j)$, where p, q, the adicity of E_i, and the

adicity of E_j are all restricted so and only so as to be consistent with the definition of Join2;

(6)   A′ is of chorisis *greater by 1* than the chorisis of A, and A′ differs from A only in respect of containing one additional occurrence of some element E_i that occurs in A.

A bit of terminology is here useful. If A′ is an immediate derivative of A, then A′ is said to *result from A by an application of*

Identity, if statement (1) describes how A′ is related to A;

Negation, if statement (2) describes how A′ is related to A;

Permutation, if statement (3) describes how A′ is related to A;

Join₁ if statement (4) describes how A′ is related to A;

Join₂ if statement (5) describes how A′ is related to A;

Iteration, if statement (6) describes how A′ is related to A; and

Junction, if either statement (4) or statement (5) describes how A′ is related to A.

Collectively, these operations will be called the Peircean *Operations of Derivation* (or: of *Construction*).

With this definition of immediate derivation, we may define Peircean *derivation* (or: *construction*) in general. We say that *an assembly B is a derivative of an assembly A* if and only if there is a finite sequence of assemblies A = $A_0, A_1, \ldots, A_k$ = B such that each A_i in the sequence, for $1 \leq i \leq k$, is an immediate derivative of A_{i-1}. Such a finite sequence of assemblies is said to be a *derivation* (or: a *construction*) *of B from A*. The number k will be said to be the *length* of the derivation.

We may now explicate the notion that a term of PAL is constructible from elements (for example, primitive terms) of PAL, and thereby the notion that a relation is constructible from other relations.

Definition 5.1: A term t of PAL is *constructible from* a set of elements $\mathbf{E} = \{E_1, E_2, \ldots, E_m\}$ if and only if: there is an assembly A = $[E_{i(1)}, E_{i(2)}, \ldots, E_{i(k)}]$ consisting of elements of **E**, *and* t is an array of some assembly B that is a derivative of A.

Definition 5.2: A term t of PAL is *reducible* if and only if t is constructible from a set of elements **E** each member of which is of adicity strictly less than the adicity of t. If t is constructible from a set of elements $\mathbf{E} = \{E_1,$

$E_2, \ldots, E_m$}, each of which is of adicity strictly less than the adicity of t, then t is said to be *reducible to the elements in* **E**.

The following Proposition is quite similar to Corollary 4.1.2.

Proposition 5.1: Suppose that a term t of PAL is constructible from a set of primitive terms of PAL $\mathbf{P} = \{R_1{}^{n_1}, R_2{}^{n_2}, \ldots, R_m{}^{n_m}\}$; and let ι, γ be any two Interpretations such that $\iota(R_i{}^{n_i}) = \gamma(R_i{}^{n_i})$ for all i with $1 \leq i \leq m$. Then, $\iota(t) = \gamma(t)$.

Proof: We may first take note again of Corollary 4.1.1, namely that, given any k elements $E_1, E_2, \ldots, E_k$ of PAL, if $\iota(E_i) = \gamma(E_i)$ for all i, $1 \leq i \leq k$, then

$$\iota(E_1 \circ E_2 \circ \ldots \circ E_k) = \gamma(E_1 \circ E_2 \circ \ldots \circ E_k) \quad .$$

We may also usefully note again the following facts cited in the proof of Corollary 4.1.2:

(a) For any element E of PAL, if $\iota(E) = \gamma(E)$, then $\iota[NEG(E)] = \gamma[NEG(E)]$;

(b) For any element E of PAL, if $\iota(E) = \gamma(E)$, then $\iota[PERM_i{}^n(E)] = \gamma[PERM_i{}^n(E)]$;

(c) For any element E of PAL, if $\iota(E) = \gamma(E)$, then $\iota[J_1{}^{ij}(E)] = \gamma[J_1{}^{ij}(E)]$;

(d) For any elements E_1, E_2 of PAL, if $\iota(E_1) = \gamma(E_1)$ and $\iota(E_2) = \gamma(E_2)$, then $\iota[J_2{}^{ij}(E_1, E_2)] = \gamma[J_2{}^{ij}(E_1, E_2)]$.

The proof, therefore, of Proposition 5.1 is quite similar to the proof of Corollary 4.1.2. It is a straightforward induction on the length of a derivation (construction) of any element of PAL from the given set of primitive terms, and by virtue of the fact that all terms of PAL are arrays of elements.

q.e.d.

We now define constructibility and reducibility for *relations* instead of terms. (It should be noted that Definition 5.3 says nothing about *effective procedures* for constructing relations; accordingly, many people might prefer to regard the notion of constructibility Definition 5.3 defines as a notion of "weak constructibility.")

Definition 5.3: A relation $\mathfrak{R}$ is *constructible from a set of relations* $\mathbf{R} = \{\mathfrak{R}_1, \mathfrak{R}_2, \ldots, \mathfrak{R}_k\}$ if and only if: there exists an Interpretation ι of PAL, a term t of PAL, and k primitive terms of PAL $R_1{}^{n_1}, R_2{}^{n_2}, \ldots, R_k{}^{n_k}$, such that:

(1) $\iota(R_i^{n_i}) = \mathfrak{R}_i$, for all i, $1 \leq i \leq k$;

(2)   t is constructible from the set of primitive terms $\{R_1^{n_1}, R_2^{n_2}, \ldots, R_k^{n_k}\}$;

and

(3)   t expresses $\mathfrak{R}$ on ι; that is to say, $CP\{Ret[\iota(t)]\} = \mathfrak{R}$.

In other words, $\mathfrak{R}$ is constructible from **R** if and only if $\mathfrak{R}$ is expressed on some Interpretation ι by a term t that is itself constructible from a set of primitive terms that on *the same* Interpretation ι express the relations in **R**. Notice that by Proposition 5.1 any Interpretation γ that matches ι on the set of primitive terms $\{R_1^{n_1}, R_2^{n_2}, \ldots, R_k^{n_k}\}$ will match ι also on any construction from these terms and thus on t. Notice also that Definition 5.3 implies that if $\mathfrak{R}$ is constructible from a set of relations **R**, then each relation in **R** is of adicity ≥ 1, because PAL contains no primitive terms of adicity 0.

Definition 5.4: A *relation* $\mathfrak{R}$ *is reducible* if and only if it is constructible from a set of relations **R** each member of which is of adicity *strictly less than* the adicity of $\mathfrak{R}$. If $\mathfrak{R}$ is constructible from a set of relations **R** = $\{\mathfrak{R}_1, \mathfrak{R}_2, \ldots, \mathfrak{R}_k\}$, each of which is of adicity strictly less than the adicity of $\mathfrak{R}$, then $\mathfrak{R}$ is said to be *reducible to the relations in* **R**.

Proposition 5.2: A relation $\mathfrak{R}$ is constructible from or reducible to a set of relations **R** = $\{\mathfrak{R}_1, \mathfrak{R}_2, \ldots, \mathfrak{R}_k\}$ only if there is a term t of PAL and k primitive terms of PAL $R_1, R_2, \ldots, R_k$, such that (1) for all i with $1 \leq i \leq k$, $Adicity(R_i) = Adicity(\mathfrak{R}_i)$; (2) t is constructible from or reducible to $\{R_1, R_2, \ldots, R_k\}$; and (3) $Adicity(t) = Adicity(\mathfrak{R})$.

Proof: The first clause follows from clause number (1) of Definition 5.3 together with the fact that, for any term term t of PAL and any interpretation ι of PAL, we have that $\iota(t) = \mathfrak{R}$ only if $Adicity(t) = Adicity(\mathfrak{R})$. The second clause follows immediately from clause number 2 of Definition 5.3. And the third clause follows from clause (3) of Definition 5.3 together with the fact that for any term t of PAL and any Interpretation ι, t expresses $\mathfrak{R}$ on ι only if $Adicity(t) = Adicity(\mathfrak{R})$. So, the clauses of the Proposition follow simply by applying basic facts about PAL to the clauses of the definitions of constructibility and reducibility for relations.

q.e.d.

Theorem 5.1: There are no reducible 0-adic or 1-adic (monadic) terms.

Proof: The proof is obvious for 0-adic terms because no elements are of adicity strictly less than 0.

Any reducible 1-adic term would have to be constructible from a set of 0-adic elements. Now any assembly A consisting of elements of a set of 0-adic elements must have as occurrences only occurrences of elements of adicity 0. Any assembly that is immediately derivative from A must result from A by application of one of the six operations of construction. Now, if E^0 is any element of adicity 0, then NEG (E^0) is an element of adicity 0. The permutations do not apply, except trivially, to 0-adic elements; nor do either of the junction operations. Iteration merely repeats a 0-adic element. Hence, any assembly that is immediately derivative from A must contain as its elements only elements of adicity 0. By induction it follows that any assembly that is derivative from A must contain as its elements only elements of adicity 0. Thus the adicity of any such assembly is 0, and the adicity of any array in such an assembly is, accordingly, 0. And no array of adicity 0 can be a term of PAL of adicity 1.

q.e.d.

Corollary 5.1.1: There are no reducible 0-adic or 1-adic relations.

Proof: By Proposition 5.2, a relation of adicity 0 or adicity 1 would be reducible only if some term of adicity 0 or adicity 1 were reducible. By the theorem, there is no such term. We may also note here that the corollary is immediately provable, quite independently of Theorem 5.1, from the fact that PAL contains no primitive terms of adicity ≤ 0.

Theorem 5.2: There are reducible terms of all adicities n, for $n \geq 2$.

Proof: Proof is by exemplification and induction. Let P be any monadic element, for example U^1 or 0^1. Then P $\circ$ P clearly is a reducible term of adicity 2; P $\circ$ P $\circ$ P clearly is a reducible term of adicity 3; P $\circ$ P $\circ$ P $\circ$ P clearly is a reducible term of adicity 4; and so forth.

q.e.d.

Corollary 5.2.1: There are reducible relations of all adicities n, for $n \geq 2$.

Proof: Given any interpretation ι, the relations expressed on ι by the terms given in the proof of the theorem are reducible relations of adicity 2, adicity 3, adicity 4, etc., respectively.

Theorem 5.3: No term of *odd* adicity can be constructed from a set of elements all of which are of *even* adicity.

Proof: Sums and differences of even integers are even integers (note that 0 is considered as an even integer). Thus, any array consisting of elements of a set of elements exclusively of even adicities is an array whose adicity is even. The same holds with the word "array" replaced by the word "assembly." Now an application of NEG or $PERM_i^n$ to an occurrence of an element in an assembly does not change the adicity of the element-occurrence that results in the assembly. Application of $Join_1$ reduces the adicity of a single element-occurrence in an assembly by 2, and hence when applied to an element-occurrence of even adicity produces an element-occurrence of even adicity. Application of $Join_2$ to two element-occurrences of even adicities yields a single element-occurrence whose adicity is 2 less than the sum of two even numbers, and is accordingly an element of even adicity. Iterating an occurrence of an element of even adicity adds to an assembly an occurrence of an element of even adicity. Thus all the operations of construction, applied to assemblies of elements of exclusively even adicities, yield assemblies of elements of exclusively even adicities, and thus assemblies whose own adicity is even. Any array in such an assembly is likewise of the same even adicity, and hence expresses a relation of even adicity on any Interpretation. By induction the theorem follows.

q.e.d

Corollary 5.3.1: No term of odd adicity can be reduced to a set of elements of exclusively even adicities.

Corollary 5.3.2: No term of odd adicity can be constructed from a set of elements of exclusively adicity 2.

Corollary 5.3.3: No term of odd adicity can be reduced to a set of elements of exlusively adicity 2.

The proofs are obvious.

Corollary 5.3.4: No relation of odd adicity can be constructed from a set of relations all of which are of even adicity.

Corollary 5.3.5: No relation of odd adicity can be reduced to a set of relations of exclusively even adicities.

Corollary 5.3.6: No relation of odd adicity can be constructed from a set of relations of exclusively adicity 2.

Corollary 5.3.7: No relation of odd adicity can be reduced to a set of relations of exclusively adicity 2.

The proofs of the last four corollaries follow from the theorem and the first three corollaries, respectively, and from Proposition 5.2.

The following two theorems, together with the corollary to Theorem 5.5, give a precise meaning to most of the negative part of the reduction thesis of this work.

Theorem 5.4: A dyadic relation is reducible if and only if it is degenerate.

Proof: (a) (IF) A degenerate dyadic relation, as we have seen, is expressible in the form $P^1 \circ Q^1$. This means that, given a degenerate dyadic relation $\mathfrak{R}$, there are primitive terms P^1 and Q^1 and an Interpretation ι such that $CP\{Ret[\iota(P^1 \circ Q^1)]\} = \mathfrak{R}$. Now the array $P^1 \circ Q^1$ is obviously constructible from the set of terms $\{P^1, Q^1\}$. Hence $\mathfrak{R}$ is constructible from the set of relations $\{\iota(P^1), \iota(Q^1)\}$, each member of which is a relation of adicity 1 and hence of adicity strictly less than the adicity of $\mathfrak{R}$. Hence $\mathfrak{R}$ is reducible.

(b) (ONLY IF) Let $\mathfrak{R}$ be any reducible dyadic relation, so that $\mathfrak{R}$ is constructible from some set of exclusively monadic relations $\mathbf{R} = \{\mathfrak{R}_1, \mathfrak{R}_2, \ldots \mathfrak{R}_p\}$. Now, let ξ be a set of primitive terms of PAL $\{R_1, R_2, \ldots, R_p\}$, and let ι be an Interpretation of PAL such that each R_i expresses the corresponding $\mathfrak{R}_i$ on ι. (In other words, $\iota(R_i) = \mathfrak{R}_i$, for all i with $1 \leq i \leq p$.) Furthermore, assume that $A = [P_1, P_2, \ldots, P_n]$ is any assembly consisting of elements of ξ. It is clear that each occurrence of an element (a primitive term) in A is an occurrence of a monadic element, and hence that $Adicity(A) = Size(A)$. We now proceed to show that any assembly B that is a derivative of A and has adicity 2 also has size 2. We do this by showing that each Peircean operation of construction preserves equality between adicity and size.

In proof of this fact, which proof proceeds by induction, we shall have to argue with reference to 0-adic elements as well as monadic elements, because 0-adic elements can result from applying $Join_2$ to two monadic elements.

The fact that each Peircean operation of construction preserves equality between adicity and size at each step of any construction beginning with A is obvious with respect to Identity, Negation, and Permutation. $Join_1$ does not apply to 0-adic or monadic elements. Any application of $Join_2$ produces one occurrence of a 0-adic element from two occurrences of 1-adic elements; it thus reduces *both* adicity *and* size by 2, thus preserving equality between adicity and size. An application of Iteration produces an additional occurrence of either a 0-adic or a 1-adic element; it thus increases *both* adicity *and* size by either 0 or 1, thus preserving equality between adicity and size.

By induction we may conclude that any assembly B that is a derivative of A has its size equal to its adicity. In other words, because adicity and size are preserved equal at every step of a derivation beginning with A, it follows by induction that any assembly B that is a derivative of A has its adicity equal to its size.

Now, by hypothesis, some assembly B that is derivative from A must have in it an array β such that β expresses $\Re$ on ι. But, if an array in B is to express $\Re$ on ι, then its adicity must be 2, so that the adicity of B must be 2. But if the adicity of B is 2, then the size of B must be 2, so that any array β in B must have size 2. From Proposition 4.9 it thus follows that the relation expressed on ι by β is degenerate. By hypothesis, however, this relation is $\Re$.

q.e.d.

By way of comment on Theorem 5.4, we may take note that it might be proved, alternatively and more simply, by applying induction to conclude that any derivation beginning with A must end with an assembly B containing exclusively 0-adic and/or 1-adic elements: any such assembly is obviously such that its adicity and size are the same.

The induction hurried over in Theorem 5.4 will be presented, *mutatis mutandis*, in the proof of Theorem 5.5.

Theorem 5.5: A triadic relation is reducible if and only if it is degenerate.

Proof: (a) (IF) A degenerate triadic relation, as we have seen, may be expressed in one of the three forms:

$P^1 \circ Q^1 \circ N^1$;

$P^1 \circ R^2$;

$R^2 \circ P^1$.

In each of these three cases it follows, by an argument similar to that of the IF part of the proof of Theorem 5.4, that the relation expressed by the array is constructible from a set of relations each of which has adicity strictly less than 3.

(b) (ONLY IF) Let $\Re$ be a reducible triadic relation, so that $\Re$ reduces to a set **R** of exclusively 0-adic, monadic, and dyadic relations $\{\Re_1, \Re_2, \ldots, \Re_p\}$. Now, let ξ be a set of primitive terms $\{R_1, R_2, \ldots, R_p\}$, and let ι be an Interpretation, such that each R_i expresses on ι the corresponding $\Re_i$. (That is, $\iota(R_i) = \Re_i$, for all i, $1 \leq i \leq p$.) And let A be any assembly $[N_1, N_2, \ldots, N_q, P_1, P_2, \ldots, P_n, S_1, S_2, \ldots, S_m]$ consisting of elements of ξ.

(In this representation, the N_i represent occurrences of 0-adic elements, the P_i represent occurrences of 1-adic elements and the S_i represent occurrences of 2-adic elements.) Now the adicity of A is clearly $n + 2m$, and the size of A is $n + m$. Hence m, the number of occurrences of dyadic elements in A is given by the formula

$$m = \text{Adicity}(A) - \text{Size}(A) \quad . \quad .$$

It will now be shown that in *any* assembly B that is a derivative of A, the number of occurrences m_B of dyadic elements is given by the formula

$$m_B = \text{Adicity}(B) - \text{Size}(B) \quad .$$

The proof is by induction on the length of any derivation of B from A. To this end, let $A = A_0, A_1, A_2, \ldots, A_b = B$ be a derivation of B from A. Let us first consider *case b = 1*. In this case B is an immediate derivative of A. Therefore, B results from A by application of one of the six Peircean operations of construction. If B results from A by an application of *Identity*, *Negation*, or *Permutation*, then the adicity, size, *and* the number of occurrences of dyadic elements of B are *the same* as they are of A. Thus $m_B = \text{Adicity}(B) - \text{Size}(B)$. If B results from A by application of *Join_1*, then it results by virtue of Join_1 applying to an occurrence of a dyadic element of A, because Join_1 is undefined for 0-adic and 1-adic elements. Thus applied, Join_1 replaces an occurrence of a dyadic element with an occurrence of a 0-adic element. Thus, $\text{Adicity}(B) = \text{Adicity}(A) - 2$; $\text{Size}(B) = \text{Size}(A) - 1$; and $m_B = m_A - 1$. Thus

$$m_B = [\text{Adicity}(A) - \text{Size}(A)] - 1$$
$$= [(\text{Adicity}(B) + 2) - (\text{Size}(B) + 1)] - 1$$
$$= \text{Adicity}(B) - \text{Size}(B) \quad .$$

If B results from A by application of *Join_2*, then there are three subcases to consider.

Subcase 1: Join_2 applies to A by virtue of operating on a pair of occurrences of monadic elements. In this case, the result is that two occurrences of 1-adic elements are replaced with one occurrence of a 0-adic element. Thus, $\text{Adicity}(B) = \text{Adicity}(A) - 2$; $\text{Size}(B) = \text{Size}(A) - 2$; and $m_B = m_A$. So

$$m_B = \text{Adicity}(A) - \text{Size}(A)$$
$$= (\text{Adicity}(B) + 2) - (\text{Size}(B) + 2)$$
$$= \text{Adicity}(B) - \text{Size}(B) \quad .$$

Subcase 2: Join$_2$ applies to A by virtue of operating on a pair one of which is an occurrence of a monadic element and the other of which is an occurrence of a dyadic element. In this case, the result is that the two occurrences are replaced with one occurrence of a l-adic element. Thus, Adicity(B) = Adicity(A) − 2; Size(B) = Size(A) − 1; and $m_B = m_A − 1$. So

$$m_B = [\text{Adicity}(A) - \text{Size}(A)] - 1$$
$$= [(\text{Adicity}(B) + 2) - (\text{Size}(B) + 1)] - 1$$
$$= \text{Adicity}(B) - \text{Size}(B) \quad .$$

Subcase 3: Join$_2$ applies to A by virtue of operating on a pair of occurrences of dyadic elements. In this case the result is that the two occurrences are replaced with one occurrence of a 2-adic element. Thus, Adicity(B) = Adicity(A) − 2; Size(B) = Size(A) − 1; and $m_B = m_A − 1$. The argument henceforward proceeds exactly as with Subcase 2.

If B results from A by application of *Iteration*, then there are three subcases to consider.

Subcase 1: An occurrence of a 0-adic element is iterated. In this case Adicity(B) = Adicity(A), Size(B) = Size(A), and $m_B = m_A$. The result in this case is obvious: m_B = Adicity(B) − Size(B).

Subcase 2: An occurrence of a monadic element is iterated. In this case Adicity(B) = Adicity(A) + 1; Size(B) = Size(A) + 1; and $m_B = m_A$. Thus

$$m_B = \text{Adicity}(A) - \text{Size}(A)$$
$$= (\text{Adicity}(B) - 1) - (\text{Size}(B) - 1)$$
$$= \text{Adicity}(B) - \text{Size}(B) \quad .$$

Subcase 3: An occurrence of a dyadic element is iterated. In this case Adicity(B) = Adicity(A) + 2; Size(B) = Size(A) + 1; and $m_B = m_A + 1$. Thus

$$m_B = [\text{Adicity}(A) - \text{Size}(A)] + 1$$
$$= [(\text{Adicity}(B) - 2) - (\text{Size}(B) - 1)] + 1$$
$$= \text{Adicity}(B) - \text{Size}(B) \quad .$$

This completes the proof for *case b = 1.* We now proceed to the *induction step.*

To this end, we suppose the result is true for a derivation of length q, where q < b, and we proceed to show that the theorem is true for a derivation of length q + 1. So let $A = A_0, A_1, A_2, \ldots, A_q, A_{q+1}$ be a derivation of length q + 1 from A of A_{q+1}. By hypothesis we have that

$$m_q = \text{Adicity}(A_q) - \text{Size}(A_q) \quad ,$$

because clearly $A = A_0, A_1, A_2, \ldots, A_q$ is a derivation of length q of A_q from A. Now of course, A_{q+1} results from A_q by application of one of the six Peircean operations of construction. Henceforward, the argument proceeds exactly as with case b = 1, with "A" being replaced by "A_q", "B" being replaced by "A_{q+1}", "m_A" being replaced by "m_q", and "m_B" being replaced by "m_{q+1}".

We have now shown that in any assembly B that is a derivative of A, the number of occurrences m_B of dyadic elements in B, is given by

$$m_B = \text{Adicity}(B) - \text{Size}(B) \quad .$$

Now by hypothesis there is some assembly B that is a derivative of A and some array β in B such that β expresses $\mathfrak{R}$ on the Interpretation ι. And, by Theorem 4.3, any assembly B is such that any array β in it expresses on any Interpretation a relation that is *not* degenerate only if $\text{Size}(B) = \text{Size}(\beta) = 1$. Hence, for B to have an array in it that does not express on ι a degenerate relation, that is, for β to express $\mathfrak{R}$ on ι and for $\mathfrak{R}$ not to be degenerate, we must have that $m_B = \text{Adicity}(B) - 1$. But, because β expresses $\mathfrak{R}$ on ι, we have that $\text{Adicity}(B) = \text{Adicity}(\beta) = \text{Adicity}(\mathfrak{R}) = 3$, so that $m_B = 3 - 1 = 2$. B must therefore contain *two* occurrences of dyadic elements, so that $\text{Adicity}(B) \geq 4$. This is a contradiction. Thus $\mathfrak{R}$ is degenerate.

q.e.d.

By way of comment on Theorem 5.5, we may take note that it might be proved, alternatively and more simply, by applying induction to conclude that any derivation beginning with A must end with an assembly B containing exclusively 0-adic, 1-adic, and/or 2-adic elements: any such assembly is obviously such that in it the number of dyadic elements m is the assembly's adicity minus the assembly's size.

Corollary 5.5.1: A relation of adicity ≥ 3 is reducible to a set exclusively of 0-adic, monadic, and/or dyadic relations if and only if it is degenerate.

Proof: (a) (IF) This part of the proof is an easy extension of the IF part of the proof of Theorem 5.5.

(b) (ONLY IF) For a relation that is not degenerate to be expressed by an array in an assembly B that is a derivative of an assembly A containing occurrences exclusively of 0-adic, monadic, and/or dyadic elements, we must have that

$$m_B = \text{Adicity}(B) - 1 \quad ,$$

as the proof of Theorem 5.5 shows. Now, if $\text{Adicity}(B) = n$, then $m_B = n - 1$. This implies that B contains $n - 1$ occurrences of dyadic elements, so that

$$\text{Adicity}(B) \geq 2(n - 1) \quad .$$

Because, however, for $n \geq 3$ we have that $2(n - 1) > n$, this implies that for $n \geq 3$, $\text{Adicity}(B) > \text{Adicity}(B)$, which is a contradiction.

q.e.d.

A few comments are in order on Theorem 5.5 and its corollary. The equation

$$m_B = \text{Adicity}(B) - 1$$

can be satisfied non-contradictorily only when either $m_B = 0$ and $\text{Adicity}(B) = 1$ or when $m_B = 1$ and $\text{Adicity}(B) = 2$. This implies that the *only* relations *not* degenerate that can be constructed exclusively from 0-adic, monadic, and/or dyadic relations are *0-adic, monadic,* and *dyadic* relations. The more general equation

$$m_B = \text{Adicity}(B) - \text{Size}(B)$$

can be satisfied non-contradictorily with $\text{Adicity}(B) = 3$ only when either

$$m_B = 1 \text{ and } \text{Size}(B) = 2$$

or

$$m_B = 0 \text{ and } \text{Size}(B) = 3 \quad .$$

This implies that the *only* triadic relations that are constructible exclusively from 0-adic, monadic, and/or dyadic relations are relations expressible by one of the forms:

$$P^1 \circ R^2 \quad ;$$
$$R^2 \circ P^1 \quad ;$$
$$P^1 \circ Q^1 \circ N^1 \quad .$$

These, of course, are the degenerate triadic relations.

1. In defining the constructibility of relations, one might use in place of clause (3) the clause
   (3′), viz. t *represents* $\Re$ on ι; that is to say, $CP[\iota(t)] = \Re$. The resulting definition of constructibility, while it would be slightly different from the definition given in Definition
   5.3, would be just as servicible for proving reduction results. Using the notion of expression rather than the notion of representation in this connection simply allows us to ignore the presence of 0-adic elements in the term t, and thus makes the presentation a bit
   simpler.

6

THE EXISTENCE OF NON-DEGENERATE RELATIONS

If all relations were degenerate, then nothing in what has so far been proved would guarantee that we could not reduce all relations to relations of adicities 1 and/or 2. An aspect of the negative part of the reduction thesis of this work, however, is the thesis that monadic and dyadic relations alone provide an insufficient basis for constructing all relations. In this section, this thesis will be proved.

In light of Theorem 5.5 and Corollary 5.5.1, it is sufficient for this purpose to prove that there are relations that are *not degenerate*. We begin with a fundamental fact.

Proposition 6.1: If D is a domain of Enterpretation for PAL of cardinality 1, and if X^k is a class of k-tuples over D of adicity $k \geq 2$, then there is a class of 1-tuples X^1 over D such that $X^k = X^1 \times X^1 \times \ldots \times X^1$.

Proof: Let d be the sole member of D. Then X^k is either Z^k or else is the class of k-tuples D^k over D defined by

$$D^k = \{(d, d, \ldots, d)\} \quad .$$

In the first case, $X^k = Z^1 \times Z^1 \times \ldots \times Z^1$. In the second case, $X^k = D^1 \times D^1 \times \ldots \times D^1$, where D^1 is the class of 1-tuples $\{(d)\}$.

q.e.d.

Theorem 6.1: Let a domain of Enterpretation D have cardinality ≥ 2. Then for all non-negative integers k there are classes of k-tuples X^k over D such that it is *not the case* that there are two integers $n \geq 1$, $m \geq 1$ such that $n + m = k$ and such that X^k is a Cartesian Product $X^n \times Y^m$ of a class of n-tuples X^n over D and a class of m-tuples Y^m over D.

Proof: We may first note that no class of k-tuples X^k for $k = 0$ or $k = 1$ could be a Cartesian Product $X^n \times Y^m$ for $n \geq 1$ and $m \geq 1$, because any such Cartesian Product must have adicity ≥ 2. Hence, the result is immediate for $k = 0$ and $k = 1$, so that we may confine our attention to $k \geq 2$. Hence, let k be ≥ 2 and let a and b be two different members of D. Then, for each $k \geq 2$ let the class of k-tuples X^k consist simply of the two k-tuples (a, a, . . . , a) and (b, b, . . . , b). Now, if X^k were a Cartesian Product $X^n \times Y^m$, with $n \geq 1$ and $m \geq 1$, then because X^k has more than one member, it must be the case that either X^n has more than one member or that Y^m

has more than one member. Without loss of generality, we may assume that Y^m has more than one member.

Therefore, given any n-tuple $(x_1, x_2, \ldots, x_n)$ in X^n, there must be *more than one* k-tuple in X^k whose first n entries are $x_1, x_2, \ldots, x_n$. That is to say, there must be in X^k at least *two* k-tuples whose first n entries are the same as each other's. But, obviously, X^k is such that, for no n with $1 \leq n \leq k$ does X^k contain at least two k-tuples whose first n entries are the same as each other's. Thus, X^k is not the Cartesian Product in question.

q.e.d.

Corollary 6.1.1: Let a domain of Enterpretation D have cardinality ≥ 2. Then, for all integers $k \geq 0$, there are classes X^k of k-tuples over D such that there do not exist any integers $n_1, n_2, \ldots, n_j$ with each $n_i \geq 1$ and with X^k being a Cartesian Product $X_1^{n_1} \times X_2^{n_2} \times \ldots \times X_j^{n_j}$ of j classes of n-tuples over D.

Proof: Because each such Cartesian Product is a Cartesian Product of its first factor and of the Cartesian Product of all its remaining factors, the Corollary follows immediately from the Theorem.

Corollary 6.1.2: Let a domain of Enterpretation D have cardinality ≥ 2. Then, for all integers $k \geq 0$, there are classes X^k of k-tuples over D such that there do not exist any integers $n_1, n_2, \ldots, n_j$ with each n_i such that $1 \leq n_i \leq 2$ and with X^k being a Cartesian Product $X_1^{n_1} \times X_2^{n_2} \times \ldots \times X_j^{n_j}$ of j classes of n-tuples over D.

Proof: This result is immediate from Corollary 6.1.1.

We now proceed to strengthen these results considerably.

Theorem 6.2: Let a domain of Enterpretation D have cardinality ≥ 2. And for each integer k with $k \geq 2$, let I^k be the set of all k-tuples over D of the form $(d, d, \ldots, d)$, with of course d a member of D. (This is just the I^k of Section 3 of this work.) Then there do not exist any two integers $n \geq 1$ and $m \geq 1$ such that I^k is a Cartesian Product $X^n \times Y^m$ of a class X^n of n-tuples over D and a class Y^m of m-tuples over D.

Proof: We may note that I^k as defined must have at least two members. We may also note that for any n with $1 \leq n \leq k$, I^k does not contain at least two k-tuples whose first n entries are the same as each other's.

Hence the proof duplicates the main part of the proof of Theorem 6.1, except that in place of "X^k" we write "I^k".

q.e.d.

Corollary 6.2.1: Given the hypothesis of Theorem 6.2 and I^k as therein defined, there do not exist any integers $n_1, n_2, \ldots, n_j$ with each $n_i \geq 1$ and with I^k being a Cartesian Product $X_1^{n_1} \times X_2^{n_2} \times \ldots \times X_j^{n_j}$ of j classes of n-tuples over D.

Proof: The proof duplicates the proof of Corollary 6.1.1 with "X^k" replaced by "I^k".

Corollary 6.2.2: Given the hypothesis of Theorem 6.2 and I^k as therein defined, there do not exist any integers $n_1, n_2, \ldots, n_j$ with each n_i such that $1 \leq n_i \leq 2$ and with I^k being a Cartesian Product $X_1^{n_1} \times X_2^{n_2} \times \ldots \times X_j^{n_j}$ of j classes of n-tuples over D.

Proof: Immediate from Corollary 6.2.1.

Theorem 6.3: Let a domain of Enterpretation D have cardinality ≥ 2. And for each k with $k \geq 2$ let I^k be defined as in Theorem 6.2. Furthermore, let the complement of I^k be written as $\langle I^k \rangle$, as in Section 3 of this work. Then it is *not the case* that there are two integers $n \geq 1$, $m \geq 1$ such that $n + m = k$ and such that $\langle I^k \rangle$ is a Cartesian Product $X^n \times Y^m$ of a class of n-tuples X^n over D and a class of m-tuples Y^m over D.

Proof: Assume that $\langle I^k \rangle$ is such a Cartesian Product, contrary to the Theorem. Now, let a and b be two distinct members of D. Then it is clear that the k-tuple (a, a, . . . , a, b) is a member of $\langle I^k \rangle$, because not all of its entries are the same. Then, by the assumption, it follows that the n-tuple (a, a, . . . , a) is a member of X^n. It is also clear that the k-tuple (b, a, a, . . . , a) is a member of $\langle I^k \rangle$, because not all of *its* entries are the same. By the assumption again, it follows that the m-tuple (a, a, . . . , a) is a member of Y^m. But, by applying the assumption a third time, it follows that the k-tuple (a, a, . . . , a) must be a member of $\langle I^k \rangle$. Because, however, all the entries of this k-tuple are the same, it is a member of I^k. This is a contradiction.

q.e.d.

Corollary 6.3.1: Let a domain of Enterpretation D have cardinality ≥ 2. And for each k with $k \geq 2$ let I^k be defined as in Theorem 6.2. Furthermore, let the complement of I^k be written as $\langle I^k \rangle$, as in Section 3 of this work. Then there do not exist any integers $n_1, n_2, \ldots, n_j$ with each n_i such that

$n_i \geq 1$ and with $\langle I^k \rangle$ being a Cartesian Product $X_1{}^{n_1} \times X_2{}^{n_2} \times \ldots \times X_j{}^{n_j}$ of j classes of n-tuples over D.

Proof: The proof duplicates, with minor differences, that of Corollary 6.1.1.

Corollary 6.3.2: Let a domain of Enterpretation D have cardinality ≥ 2. And for each k with $k \geq 2$ let I^k be defined as in Theorem 6.2. Furthermore, let the complement of I^k be written as $\langle I^k \rangle$, as in Section 3 of this work. Then there do not exist any integers $n_1, n_2, \ldots, n_j$ with each n_i such that $1 \leq n_i \leq 2$ and with $\langle I^k \rangle$ being a Cartesian Product $X_1{}^{n_1} \times X_2{}^{n_2} \times \ldots \times X_j{}^{n_j}$ of j classes of n-tuples over D.

Proof: The proof duplicates, with minor differences, that of Corollary 6.1.2.

Therorem 6.4: On the assumption that the model structure $M = (W, D)$ for PAL contains at least one domain D_w of cardinality ≥ 2, it follows that for all $k \geq 2$ the relation ID^k, denoted by the term 1^k, is non-degenerate. (Recall that we must have $k \geq 2$ for the term 1^k to be a primitive term of PAL.)

Proof: Obvious from the definition of a degenerate relation and from Corollary 6.2.2.

Theorem 6.5: On the assumption that the model structure $M = (W, D)$ for PAL contains at least one domain D_w of cardinality ≥ 2, it follows that for all $k \geq 2$ the relation denoted by the term $NEG(1^k)$ is non-degenerate. (Recall that we must have $k \geq 2$ for the term 1^k to be a primitive term of PAL.)

Proof: Obvious from the definition of a degenerate relation and from Corollary 6.3.2.

7

TERIDENTITY, THE COMMA OPERATOR, AND DERIVED ELEMENTS

We have now seen that, starting from monadic and dyadic relations exclusively, we are limited as to the relations of higher adicities that we can construct (in the sense of this work). Whatever relations of adicity three or higher that we can construct from monadic and dyadic relations alone are all degenerate relations, whereas there are non-degenerate—indeed, non-composite—relations of all adicities. What will be shown in the remainder of this work is that when we allow ourselves to use *triadic* relations in addition to monadic and dyadic ones in beginning our constructions, all limitation as to the relations we can construct vanishes.

Among non-degenerate triadic relations, as we have seen, is the *teridentity* relation ID^3, denoted by 1^3. This relation assumes a central role in the proof of the Peirce-inspired reduction thesis of this work. Teridentity is also the key to understanding the consistency of this thesis with the various "reductions to dyadic relations" that on their surface might appear to contradict this thesis.

In the standard logical literature, identity always appears in the guise of a dyadic relation. Teridentity, quadidentity, and so forth, thus become represented as conjunctions of dyadic identity formulae, so that ID^3 appears as x = y & y = z, ID^4 appears as x = y & y = z & z = w, and so forth.

In PAL, however, the teridentity relation ID^3 is not constructible from the dyadic identity relation ID^2 alone, or even from this relation and any other set of exclusively dyadic and/or monadic relations; the proof was given in Theorem 6.2 and its corollaries. The first theorem of this section, however, Theorem 7.1, proves that from the teridentity relation ID^3 alone we may construct ID^2 as also, indeed, ID^n for all $n \geq 3$. In other words, PAL represents identity as irreducibly triadic, in the sense that, rather than representing all identity relations of all adicities ≥ 2 as definable in terms of the dyadic identity relation, PAL represents all identity relations of all adicities not 3 as definable in terms of teridentity alone, whereas it represents identity relations of adicity 3 and greater as not being definable in terms of the dyadic identity relation alone or supplemented by other monadic and/or dyadic relations. The philosophical significance and potential philosophical justification for regarding identity as irreducibly triadic in this way rather than dyadic must remains topics for future works.

Theorem 7.1: From the set of relations consisting of the teridentity relation ID^3 alone, all the identity relations ID^n, for $n \geq 2$ may be constructed.

Proof: The primitive term 1^3 of PAL denotes (i.e. expresses on every Interpretation) the relation ID^3. Now, it is obvious that from the set of primitive terms $\{1^3\}$ the element $J_1^{23}[J_2^{34}(1^3,1^3)]$ may be constructed. We now prove that for all Interpretations ι,

$$\iota\{J_1^{23}[J_2^{34}(1^3,1^3)]\} = ID^2 \quad ,$$

so that the element $J_1^{23}[J_2^{34}(1^3,1^3)]$ denotes the relation ID^2 (that is, the element expresses this relation on all Interpretations). For this purpose, it suffices to show that for any Enterpretation $(D,*)$, $*\{J_1^{23}[J_2^{34}(1^3,1^3)]\}$ is the class of 2-tuples I^2 over D consisting of every 2-tuple (d,d) such that d is a member of D. So, let $(D,*)$ be any Enterpretation of PAL. Then,

$$*[J_2^{34}(1^3,1^3)] = SD^{34}[*(1^3) \times *(1^3)]$$
$$= DEL^{34}\{SEL^{34}[*(1^3) \times *(1^3)]\} \quad .$$

But $*(1^3)$ = the class of all 3-tuples I^3 over D consisting of every 3-tuple (d,d,d) such that d is a member of D. Hence,

$$*(1^3) \times *(1^3) = X^6 \quad ,$$

where X^6 is the class of all 6-tuples (d,d,d,e,e,e), with d and e being members of D. Now, clearly, $SEL^{34}(X^6) = I^6$, where I^6 is the class of all 6-tuples over D consisting of every 6-tuple (d,d,d,d,d,d) for d a member of D. Moreover, $DEL^{34}(I^6) = I^4$, where I^4 is the class of 4-tuples over D consisting of every 4-tuple (d,d,d,d) for d a member of D. So,

$$SD^{34}[*(1^3) \times *(1^3)] = I^4 \quad .$$

It follows that

$$*\{J_1^{23}[J_2^{34}(1^3,1^3)]\} = SD^{23}(I^4) \quad .$$

But $SEL^{23}(I^4) = I^4$, and $DEL^{23}(I^4) = I^2$, so that $SD^{23}(I^4) = I^2$. Hence,

$$*\{J_1^{23}[J_2^{34}(1^3,1^3)]\} = I^2 \quad .$$

Now that we have shown that the dyadic identity relation ID^2 is constructible from the teridienty relation, we proceed to the rest of the theorem.

We shall now show that ID^{n+1} may be constructed from ID^3 and ID^n for all $n \geq 2$. For this it suffices to show that for all Enterpretations $(D,*)$, and for all $n \geq 2$, the element $J_2{}^{34}(1^3,1^n)$, which is obviously constructible from the set of primitive terms $\{1^3,1^n\}$, is such that $*[J_2{}^{34}(1^3,1^n)] = I^{n+1}$. So, let $(D,*)$ be any Enterpretation of PAL. Then $*(1^3) \times *(1^n)$ is the class of all $(n+3)$-tuples $(d,d,d,e,e, \ldots ,e)$ with d and e being members of D. Call this class X^{n+3}. Now, because $SEL^{34}(X^{n+3}) = I^{n+3}$, and $DEL^{34}(I^{n+3}) = I^{n+1}$, it follows that $SD^{34}(X^{n+3}) = I^{n+1}$. Hence, $*[J_2{}^{34}(1^3,1^n)] = I^{n+1}$. It follows that on any Interpretation ι, $\iota[J_2{}^{34}(1^3,1^n)] = ID^{n+1}$, so that the term $J_2{}^{34}(1^3,1^n)$ denotes the relation ID^{n+1}.

The theorem now follows by induction.

q.e.d.

Corollary 7.1.1: For all Enterpretations $(D,*)$, and for all $1 \leq i \leq n < j \leq n+m$,

$$*[J_2{}^{ij}(1^n,1^m)] = *(1^{n+m-2}) \quad .$$

Consequently, for all Interpretations , and for all $1 \leq i \leq n < j \leq n+m$,

$$\iota[J_2{}^{ij}(1^n,1^m)] = \iota(1^{n+m-2}) = ID^{n+m-2} \quad .$$

Proof: By obvious generalization of the last paragraph in the proof of Theorem 7.1.

q.e.d.

Theorem 7.2: From the set of relations consisting of the teridentity relation ID^3 alone, the universal relations $UNIV^n$, for all $n \geq 1$, denoted by U^n for all $n \geq 1$, respectively, may be constructed.

Proof: We first show that $UNIV^1$ may be constructed from the teridentity relation ID^3. For this, it suffices to show that for all Enterpretations $(D,*)$, the element $J_1{}^{12}(1^3)$, which is obviously constructible from the set of primitive terms $\{1^3\}$, is such that $*[J_1{}^{12}(1^3)] = V^1$, the class of all 1-tuples over D excluding the null 1-tuple. This is easily verified by using the methods of the previous theorem. Thus, the element $J_1{}^{12}(1^3)$ expresses $UNIV^1$ on every Interpretation.

Now it is obvious that $UNIV^{n+1}$ is expressed on any Interpretation by the array $U^1 \circ U^n$. But, because U^1 and $J_1{}^{12}(1^3)$ both express the same relation, namely $UNIV^1$, on every Interpretation, the theorem follows by induction. Alternatively, we may note that the array of chorisis n

$$J_1{}^{12}(1^3) \circ J_1{}^{12}(1^3) \circ \ldots \circ J_1{}^{12}(1^3) \quad ,$$

which is obviously constructible from $\{1^3\}$, expresses $UNIV^n$ on every Interpretation.

q.e.d.

Recall from Theorem 7.1 that ID^2 may be constructed from teridentity alone. And take note that, as is easily verified, the relation TRUE is denoted (that is, expressed on every Interpretation) by the element $J_1^{12}(1^2)$. These facts hint at the following theorem.

Theorem 7.3: From the set of relations consisting of the teridentity relation ID^3 alone, the 0-adic relations FALSE and TRUE may be constructed.

Proof: The element $J_1^{12}\{J_1^{23}[J_2^{34}(1^3,1^3)]\}$ is obviously constructible from the set of primitive terms $\{1^3\}$. Moreover, as the proof of Theorem 7.1 hints: for all Enterpretations $(D,*)$, we have that

$$*[J_1^{12}\{J_1^{23}[J_2^{34}(1^3,1^3)]\}] = *[J_1^{12}(1^2)] = \mathsf{T} \quad .$$

It follows that, on any Interpretation ι,

$$\iota[J_1^{12}\{J_1^{23}[J_2^{34}(1^3,1^3)]\}] = \text{TRUE} \quad .$$

It obviously follows also, moreover, that

$NEG[J_1^{12}\{J_1^{23}[J_2^{34}(1^3,1^3)]\}]$ denotes FALSE. The result, therefore, is obvious.

q.e.d.

Theorem 7.4: From the set of relations consisting of the teridentity relation ID^3 alone, all the null relations $NULL^n$, for $n \geq 1$, denoted by 0^n for $n \geq 1$ respectively, may be constructed.

Proof: $UNIV^1$, as Theorem 7.2 shows, may be constructed from teridentity alone. Moreover, it is easily seen that $NEG(U^1)$ denotes $NULL^1$. Thus, the element $NEG[J_1^{12}(1^3)]$, which is obviously constructible from $\{1^3\}$, denotes $NULL^1$.

Now, $NULL^2$ is denoted by the array $0^1 \circ U^1$; and, in general, the relation $NULL^{n+1}$ is denoted by the array $0^1 \circ U^n$ for all $n \geq 1$. This fact should make it clear that the theorem follows by induction.

q.e.d.

The following comment is in order on Theorem 7.4. Because $NULL^n$ is the negation of the relation $UNIV^n$, one might mistakenly think that we could prove the constructibility of $NULL^n$ from $\{ID^3\}$ by citing the fact that $NEG(U^n)$ denotes $NULL^n$ and the fact that $UNIV^n$ is constructible from teridentity alone. Unfortunately, this line of thought is incorrect: we do not yet have in PAL resources for negating arrays of chorisis ≥ 2; NEG applies only to *elements*. Because, therefore, $UNIV^n$, for $n \geq 2$, has been constructed only as being expressed by an array of chorisis ≥ 2, and because we may not apply NEG to such an array of PAL, we may not try to apply NEG to U^n for $n \geq 2$ in order to justify the construction of $NULL^n$ from teridentity alone. We shall later be able to treat arrays of chorisis ≥ 2 as if they were single elements, and this will be the key to the positive part of the reduction thesis of this work. But for the moment, this treatment of arrays of chorisis ≥ 2 is not available.

Two Propositions concerning constructibility are now in order.

Proposition 7.1: Every 0-adic relation may be constructed from dyadic relations alone.

Proof: A 0-adic relation is a function $\Re$ such that, for any w in W, $\Re(w) = \top$ or $\Re(w) = \bot$. Given, therefore, any 0-adic relation $\Re$, define the dyadic relation ψ such that $\psi(w) = V^2$ (the class of all 2-tuples over D_w excluding the null 2-tuple over D_w) if $\Re(w) = \top$ and $\psi(w) = Z^2$ (the class containing only the null 2-tuple over D_w) if $\Re(w) = \bot$. Now, let R^2 be a primitive term of PAL and let ι be an Interpretation of PAL such that $\iota(R^2) = \psi$. Then it is easily verified that $\iota[J_1^{12}(R^2)] = \Re$. Hence, $\Re$ is constructible from $\{\psi\}$.

q.e.d.

Proposition 7.2: Every monadic relation may be constructed from triadic relations alone.

Proof: A monadic relation is a function $\Re$ such that, for any w in W, $\Re(w)$ is a class of 1-tuples over D_w. Given, therefore, any 1-adic relation $\Re$, define the triadic relation ψ such that $\psi(w)$ contains the 3-tuple (a,a,a) if and only if $\Re(w)$ contains the 1-tuple (a); also such that $\psi(w) = Z^3$ (the class containing only the null 3-tuple over D_w) if $\Re(w) = Z^1$ (the class containing only the null 1-tuple over D_w). Now, let R^3 be a primitive term of PAL and let ι be an Interpretation of PAL such that $\iota(R^3) = \psi$. Then it is easily verified that $\iota[J_1^{23}(R^3)] = \Re$. Hence, $\Re$ is constructible from $\{\psi\}$.

q.e.d.

For the proof of the Representation Theorem in the following section of this work, we shall need to be able to perform within PAL all the operations of quantificational logic (that is, first order predicate logic with identity). With teridentity available we shall be able to do this, whereas otherwise it is impossible. In particular, we shall now undertake to introduce several operations on relations by means of defining corresponding operations on terms of PAL. As we shall see, these operations are defined from the Peircean operations of construction *together with* the primitive term 1^3. These operations will be referrred to as the *derived operations of PAL*. As operations on terms of PAL, they all have the effect of producing *elements* of PAL as the result of their application. Elements produced by the derived operations will be called *derived elements* of PAL. The significance of these operations at the level of semantics, both extensional and intensional, will be explicated along with the operations themselves.

The first, and probably the most important, of these derived operations will be called the *Comma Operator*. The comma operator is a brilliant device that Peirce was using with great skill and effect at least as early as 1870.[1] At the level of semantics, if $n \geq 1$, the comma operator has the effect of "doubling up" one of the columns (column-vectors) of a class X^n of n-tuples over a domain D or one of the "adicity places" or "hooks" of a relation $\Re$ of adicity n; the comma operator yields thereby a class of $(n + 1)$-tuples over D, or a relation of adicity $n + 1$, which class, or which relation, nevertheless, is in a certain sense the same in significance as X^n or as $\Re$. In the case, for example, of a monadic relation expressed on some Interpretation by the primitive term P^1 and given in quantificational logic by, say, $P(x)$, the comma operator's effect is to yield the dyadic relation given in quantificational logic by $R(x,y)$, where $R(x,y)$ is defined by $P(x)$ & $x = y$. In the case of terms of adicity ≥ 2, the comma operator will have to be indexed (superscripted) to show *which* "adicity place" or "hook" it is to be taken as "doubling up." Accordingly, the comma operator will *in general* be superscripted. If, therefore, $n \geq 1$, and we have an n-adic relation $\Re$ that is expressed on some Interpretation by the primitive term R^n; and if R^n has the comma operator, indexed (i.e., superscripted) by i with $1 \leq i \leq n$, applied to it; then the result at the level of intensional semantics is an $(n + 1)$-adic relation in which the ith "hook" of $\Re$ is "doubled up." If the n-adic relation is given in quantificational logic by $R(x_1, x_2, \ldots, x_n)$, then the result of applying the i-indexed comma operator is given in quantificational logic by the $(n + 1)$-adic relation $S(x_1, x_2, \ldots, x_n, x_{n+1})$, where $S(x_1, x_2, \ldots, x_n, x_{n+1})$ is defined as

$$R(x_1, x_2, \ldots, x_i, x_{i+2}, \ldots, x_{n+1}) \ \& \ x_i = x_{i+1} \quad .$$

The i-indexed comma operator will be written as

COMMA^i

and defined so that if the argument is an element of adicity 0, then $i = 0$, and if the argument is an element of adicity $n \geq 1$, then $1 \leq i \leq n$. In general, the comma operator may be defined in terms of the junction operations, certain permutation operations, and the term 1^3 that denotes the teridentity relation. Let us begin by picking out, from among the permuation operations $PERM_i^n$ certain cycle operations. Specifically, let $CYCLE(n)^i$, for $1 \leq i \leq n$, be the permutation operation corresponding to the permutation

$$\begin{pmatrix} 1, 2, 3, \ldots, i-1, & i, & i+1, & \ldots, n \\ 1, 2, 3, \ldots, i-1, i+1, & \ldots, & n-1, n, i \end{pmatrix} \quad ,$$

which cycles the last $n - i + 1$ entries in the list and is a cycle of length $n - i + 1$. Specifically, $Cycle(n)^i$ moves whatever is in the last (that is, the nth) position to the ith position while shifting whatever is in positions i through $n - 1$ one place to the right. We are now ready for the first part of the definition of the Comma Operator.

Definition 7.1a: By definition, for any element E^n of adicity $n \geq 1$ and for $1 \leq i \leq n$, $COMMA^i(E^n)$ is the element

$$CYCLE(n + 1)^{i + 1}\{CYCLE(n + 1)^i[J_2^{i,n + 1}(E^n, 1^3)]\} \quad .$$

Given any Enterpretation $(D, *)$, and given that $n \geq 1$, if $*(E^n) = Z^n$, the class containing only the null n-tuple over D, then for all i with $1 \leq i \leq n$, $*[COMMA^i(E^n)] = Z^{n + 1}$, the class containing only the null $(n + 1)$-tuple over D. It follows that, if E^n expresses on some Interpretation ι the n-adic null relation $NULL^n$ (that is to say, if $\iota(E^n) = NULL^n$), then $COMMA^i(E^n)$ expresses on ι, for all i with $1 \leq i \leq n$, the $(n + 1)$-adic null relation $NULL^{n + 1}$ (that is to say, $\iota[COMMA^i(E^n)] = NULL^{n + 1}$). Similarly, if E^n expresses on some Interpretation ι the n-adic identity relation ID^n (that is to say, if $\iota(E^n) = ID^n$), then $COMMA^i(E^n)$ expresses on ι, for all i with $1 \leq i \leq n$ and $n \geq 2$, the $(n + 1)$-adic identity relation $ID^{n + 1}$ (that is to say, $\iota[COMMA^i(E^n)] = ID^{n + 1}$). If $n \geq 2$, then $COMMA^i(1^n)$ denotes the relation $ID^{n + 1}$. Also, $COMMA^1(U^1)$ denotes ID^2.

At the level of extensional semantics, if $n \geq 1$, $COMMA^i$ has the effect of doubling up the ith column of the matrix corresponding to E^n, for $n \geq 1$, so that if $(D, *)$ is any Enterpretation of PAL and if

$$*(E^n) = \{(\delta_1, \delta_2, \ldots, \delta_i, \delta_{i + 1}, \ldots, \delta_n)\} \quad ,$$

then

$$*[\text{COMMA}^i(E^n)] = \{(\delta_1, \delta_2, \ldots, \delta_i, \delta_i, \delta_{i+1}, \ldots, \delta_n)\}$$.

This fact may be directly verified from the definitions.

At the level of intensional semantics, if $n \geq 1$, COMMA^i has the effect of doubling up the ith column of each matrix corresponding to E^n for each w in W.

It might be remarked at this point that COMMA^i could also have been defined in terms of the cycle operation $\text{CYCLE}(n,i)$, which is defined for $1 \leq i \leq n$ to be the permutation operation corresponding to the permutation

$$\begin{pmatrix} 1, 2, 3, \ldots, i-1, i, i+1, \ldots, n \\ 1, 2, 3, \ldots, i-1, n, i, i+1, \ldots, n-1 \end{pmatrix} ,$$

which, like $\text{CYCLE}(n)^i$, cycles the last $n-i+1$ entries in the list and is a cycle of length $n-i+1$. But $\text{CYCLE}(n,i)$ moves whatever is in the ith position to the last (that is, the nth) position, while shifting whatever is in positions $i+1$ through n one place to the left. Using this operation, $\text{COMMA}^i(E^n)$ could be defined as the result of $n-i$ applications of $\text{CYCLE}(n+1,i)$ to the term $J_2^{i,n+1}(E^n,1^3)$.

Even though we have not yet introduced the comma operator in connection with elements of adicity 0, two more Propositions are in order at this point.

Proposition 7.3: Every dyadic relation may be constructed from triadic relations alone.

Proof: A dyadic relation is a function $\Re$ such that, for any w in W, $\Re(w)$ is a class of 2-tuples over D_w. Given, therefore, any 2-adic relation $\Re$, define the triadic relation ψ such that $\psi(w)$ contains the 3-tuple (a,b,b) if and only if $\Re(w)$ contains the 2-tuple (a,b); also such that $\psi(w) = Z^3$ (the class containing only the null 3-tuple over D_w) if $\Re(w) = Z^2$ (the class containing only the null 2-tuple over D_w). Now, let R^3 be a primitive term of PAL and let ι be an Interpretation of PAL such that $\iota(R^3) = \psi$. Then it is easily verified that $\iota\{J_1^{34}[\text{COMMA}^3(R^3)]\} = \Re$. It follows that $\Re$ is constructible from $\{\psi, \text{ID}^3\}$. It may be noted that the relation ID^3 is included in this set of relations because it is required for constructing the comma operator.

q.e.d.

Proposition 7.4: Every 0-adic relation may be constructed from triadic relations alone.

Proof: A 0-adic relation is a function $\Re$ such that, for any w in W, $\Re(w) = \mathsf{T}$ or $\Re(w) = \perp$. Given, therefore, any 0-adic relation $\Re$, define the triadic relation ψ such that $\psi(w) = V^3$ (the class of all 3-tuples over Dw excluding the null 3-tuple) if $\Re(w) = \mathsf{T}$ and $\psi(w) = Z^3$ (the class containing only the null 3- tuple) if $\Re(w) = \perp$. Now, let R^3 be a primitive term of PAL and let ι be an Interpretation of PAL such that $\iota(R^3) = \psi$. Then it is easily verified that $\iota[J_1{}^{12}\{J_1{}^{34}[\text{COMMA}^3(R^3)]\}] = \Re$. It follows that $\Re$ is constructible from $\{\psi, \text{ID}^3\}$. ID^3 is included in this set of relations because it is required for constructing the comma operator.

q.e.d.

At this point, we are ready to define the comma operator COMMA^0 for elements of PAL of adicity 0. We recall that there are no *primitive* terms of PAL of adicity 0 and that, accordingly, every element of adicity 0 has either the form $J_1{}^{12}(E^2)$, for E^2 an element of adicity 2, or else the form $J_2{}^{12}(E^1,F^1)$, for E^1 and F^1 both elements of adicity 1. Recalling this fact prepares us for the second part of the definition of the Comma Operator.

Definition 7.1.b: COMMA^0 is defined as follows: (a) if E^0 has the form $J_1{}^{12}(E^2)$, then $\text{COMMA}^0(E^0) = \text{COMMA}^0[J_1{}^{12}(E^2)]$ is the element $J_1{}^{12}[J_2{}^{13}(E^2,1^3)]$; and (b) if E^0 has the form $J_2{}^{12}(E^1,F^1)$, then $\text{COMMA}^0(E^0) = \text{COMMA}^0[J_2{}^{12}(E^1,F^1)]$ is the element $J_2{}^{13}[J_2{}^{12}(E^1,1^3),F^1]$.

Two Propositions about the comma operator as applied to 0-adic elements are now in order.

Proposition 7.5: If E^0 is a 0-adic element of PAL, then for any Enterpretation $(D,*)$, $*[\text{COMMA}^0(E^0)] = Z^1$ if and only if $*(E^0) = \perp$. (Z^1 is, of course, the class of 1-tuples over D containing only the null 1-tuple.) And, because $*(E^0)$ must be either T or $\perp$, it follows immediately that $*[\text{COMMA}^0(E^0)] \neq Z^1$ if and only if $*(E^0) = \mathsf{T}$.

Proof: (Part 1) Assume that E^0 is of the form $J_1{}^{12}(E^2)$ for some element E^2 of adicity 2 of PAL. Then:

If $*(E^0) = \perp$, then $*[J_1{}^{12}(E^2)] = \perp$, so that $SD^{12}[*(E^2)] = \perp$. This means that $*(E^2)$ contains no 2-tuple whose first and second entries are the same member of D. Now $*[\text{COMMA}^0(E^0)] = *\{J_1{}^{12}[J_2{}^{13}(E^2,1^3)]\} = SD^{12}\{SD^{13}[*(E^2) \times *(1^3)]\}$. But $*(E^2) \times *(1^3) =$ the class of all 5-tuples over D of the form (a,b,c,c,c) with (a,b) in $*(E^2)$ and c a member of D. It follows that $SD^{13}[*(E^2) \times *(1^3)] =$ the class of all 3-tuples over D of the form (b,a,a) with (a,b) in $*(E^2)$. Therefore, because $*(E^2)$ contains no

2-tuple whose first and second entries are the same member of D, it follows that $SEL^{12}\{SD^{13}[*(E^2) \times *(1^3)]\} = Z^3$. Hence $SD^{12}\{SD^{13}[*(E^2) \times *(1^3)]\} = Z^1$.

Conversely, if $*[COMMA^0(E^0)] = *\{J_1{}^{12}[J_2{}^{13}(E^2,1^3)]\} = SD^{12}\{SD^{13}[*(E^2) \times *(1^3)]\} = Z^1$, then $SD^{13}[*(E^2) \times *(1^3)]$ contains no 3-tuple over D whose first and second entries are the same member of D. But, because $SD^{13}[*(E^2) \times *(1^3)] =$ the class of all 3-tuples over D of the form (b,a,a) with (a,b) in $*(E^2)$, it follows that there are no 2-tuples in $*(E^2)$ whose first and second entries are the same member of D. So, $*(E^0) = *[J_1{}^{12}(E^2)] = DEL^{12}\{SEL^{12}[*(E^2)]\} = DEL^{12}(Z^2) = \perp$.

(Part 2) Assume that E^0 is of the form $J_2{}^{12}(E^1,F^1)$ for some element E^1 and some element F^1 of PAL, both of adicity 1. Then:

If $*(E^0) = \perp$, then $*[J_2{}^{12}(E^1,F^1)] = \perp$, so that $SD^{12}[*(E^1) \times *(F^1)] = \perp$. Thus, $SEL^{12}[*(E^1) \times *(F^1)] = Z^2$; that is to say, $*(E^1)$ and $*(F^1)$ have no 1-tuple over D in common with each other. Now, $*[COMMA^0(E^0)] = *\{COMMA^0[J_2{}^{12}(E^1,F^1)]\} = *\{J_2{}^{13}[J_2{}^{12}(E^1,1^3),F^1]\} = SD^{13}\{*[J_2{}^{12}(E^1,1^3)] \times *(F^1)\}$. But $*[J_2{}^{12}(E^1,1^3)] = SD^{12}[*(E^1) \times *(1^3)] =$ the class of all 2-tuples over D of the form (e,e) with (e) in $*(E^1)$. Hence, $*\{J_2{}^{13}[J_2{}^{12}(E^1,1^3),F^1]\} = SD^{13}(X^3)$, where X^3 is the class of all 3-tuples over D of the form (e,e,f), where (e) is in $*(E^1)$ and (f) is in $*(F^1)$. But, because $*(E^1)$ and $*(F^1)$ have no 1-tuples in common, $SEL^{13}(X^3) = Z^3$, so that $SD^{13}(X^3) = Z^1$.

Conversely, if $*[COMMA^0(E^0)] = *\{COMMA^0[J_2{}^{12}(E^1,F^1)]\} = *\{J_2{}^{13}[J_2{}^{12}(E^1,1^3),F^1]\} = SD^{13}\{*[J_2{}^{12}(E^1,1^3)] \times *(F^1)\} = Z^1$, then—because $*[J_2{}^{12}(E^1,1^3)] = SD^{12}[*(E^1) \times *(1^3)] =$ the class of all 2-tuples over D of the form (e,e) with (e) in $*(E^1)$—it follows that $*[J_2{}^{12}(E^1,1^3)] \times *(F^1) = X^3$, where X^3 is the class of all 3-tuples over D of the form (e,e,f), with (e) in $*(E^1)$ and (f) in $*(F^1)$. Because $SD^{13}(X^3) = Z^1$, it follows that $SEL^{13}(X^3) = Z^3$ and thus that $*(E^1)$ and $*(F^1)$ have no 1-tuple in common. Consequently, $SD^{12}[*(E^1) \times *(F^1)] = \perp$, so that $*(E^0) = *[J_2{}^{12}(E^1,F^1)] = \perp$.

q.e.d.

Proposition 7.6: An element E^0 of adicity 0 of PAL is such that, for any Interpretation ι, and for all w in W, $[\iota(E^0)](w) = \perp$ if and only if $\{\iota[COMMA^0(E^0)]\}(w) = Z^1$, where Z^1 is the class of 1-tuples over D_w containing only the null 1-tuple.

Proof: Immediate from Proposition 7.5.

Having defined the comma operator, we may go on to define the (existential) quantification operator $QUANT^i$ whose effect at the semantic level is to quantify existentially with regard to the ith hook of the relation expressed by its argument, thus yielding a relation of adicity one less than its argument. Extensionally, $QUANT^i$ has the effect of deleting the ith column of the matrix corresponding to its argument (and, of course, closing the matrix up and eliminating any duplications in the rows that result); it is thus the equivalent of Bernays's "Streichung" operation and the permutations. Here is the definition.

Definition 7.2: For any element E^n, of adicity n, and for $1 \leq i \leq n$, $QUANT^i(E^n)$ is the element

$$J_1^{i,i+1}[COMMA^i(E^n)] \quad .$$

If (D,*) is any given Enterpretation for PAL, then the following assertions hold. If $n \geq 2$ and $*(E^n) = Z^n$, then $*[QUANT^i(E^n)] = Z^{n-1}$. If $n \geq 2$, and $*(E^n) \neq Z^n$, so that

$$*(E^n) = \{(\delta_1, \delta_2, \ldots, \delta_{i-1}, \delta_i, \delta_{i+1}, \ldots, \delta_n)\} \quad ,$$

then

$$*[QUANT^i(E^n)] = \{(\delta_1, \delta_2, \ldots, \delta_{i-1}, \delta_{i+1}, \ldots, \delta_n)\} \quad .$$

If $*(E^1) = Z^1$, then $*[QUANT^i(E^1)] = \perp$; and if $*(E^1) \neq Z^1$, then $*[QUANT^i(E^1)] = T$. $QUANT^i$ is undefined for 0-adic terms. These facts are easily verified from the definition. Consequently,

$$*[QUANT^i(E^n)] = DEL^i[*(E^n)] \quad .$$

The next two operators to be introduced provide in PAL resources for accomplishing the same effects that in quantificational logic are accomplished by identifying variables. In quantificational logic, variables may be identified with each other in two different ways. First, they may be identified by explicitly conjoining with a formula containing free variables x_1 and x_2 the formula

$$x_1 = x_2 \quad .$$

Second, they may be identified by using two or more occurrences of the same variable. Thus, for example, if a relation is given in quantificational logic by the formula

$$R(x_1, x_2, \ldots, x_{n-1}, x_n) \quad ,$$

where each x_i is a variable distinct from each of the others, we may identify the variables x_1 and x_{n-1} by writing the formula

$R(x_1, x_2, \ldots, x_{n-1}, x_n)$ & $x_1 = x_{n-1}$,

or we may identify these variables by writing the formula

$R(x_1, x_2, \ldots, x_1, x_n)$.

The crucial difference between the two ways of identifying variables is that the first produces a relation of the same adicity, namely n, as the original; whereas the second produces a relation of adicity 1 less than the original. This difference, of course, shows up at the semantic level of quantificational logic in the lengths of the two sets of tuples making up the interpretations of the two relations.

Corresponding to the first way of identifying variables in quantificational logic are the operators ADID, variously superscripted, of PAL. Corresponding to the second way of identifying variables in quantificational logic are the operators HOOKID, variously superscripted, of PAL. ADID and HOOKID are definable in a variety of ways, but the easiest of these is to define them first for two indices (that is, superscripts) only, and then to define them more generally by induction.

Definition 7.3: To this end, let E^n be an element of PAL of adicity $n \geq 2$. And let $1 \leq i < j \leq n$. Then, by definition, $\text{ADID}^{ij}(E^n)$ is the element

$\text{CYCLE}(n)^j\{\text{CYCLE}(n)^i[J_1^{i,n}(J_2^{j,n+1}(E^n,1^4))]\}$.

It is to be noted carefully that the order of the CYCLE operations with respect to the superscripts i and j is crucial in this definition, because $\text{CYCLE}(n)^i$ followed by $\text{CYCLE}(n)^j$, (as the definition requires) is not in general equivalent in result to $\text{CYCLE}(n)^j$ followed by $\text{CYCLE}(n)^i$.

Definition 7.4: By definition, $\text{HOOKID}^{ij}(E^n)$ is the element

$\text{CYCLE}(n-1)^i\{J_1^{i,n}[J_2^{j,n+1}(E^n,1^3)]\}$.

It is clear, from the specification $1 \leq i < j \leq n$ in the definitions of ADID and HOOKID, that these operations are undefined for elements E^n with $n = 0$ or $n = 1$.

The semantics for ADID^{ij} and for HOOKID^{ij} are as follows. It can be directly verified from the definitions that, given any Enterpretation $(D, *)$,

$*[\text{ADID}^{ij}(E^n)] = \text{SEL}^{ij}[*(E^n)]$,

which is, of course, equal to the set of all n-tuples in $*(E^n)$ that have the form

$$(d_1, d_2, \ldots, d_{i-1}, d, d_{i+1}, \ldots, d_{j-1}, d, d_{j+1}, \ldots, d_n) \quad .$$

The proof of this fact is simple but tedious to write out; it will here be omitted.

It can also be directly verified that, given any Enterpretation $(D,*)$,

$$*[HOOKID^{ij}(E^n)] = DEL^j\{SEL^{ij}[*(E^n)]\} \quad .$$

The proof, again, is simple but tedious to write out, and will be omitted.

One may take note that HOOKID may be used to reverse the effect of the COMMA operator, because, given any Enterpretation $(D,*)$,

$$*(E^n) = *\{HOOKID^{i,i+1}[COMMA^i(E^n)]\} \quad .$$

Also, because $SEL^{ij}[*(E^n)] = SEL^{ij}\{SEL^{ij}[*(E^n)]\}$, we have, for all $(D,*)$, that

$$*[HOOKID^{ij}(E^n)]$$

$$= DEL^j\{SEL^{ij}[*(E^n)]\}$$

$$= DEL^j(SEL^{ij}\{SEL^{ij}[*(E^n)]\})$$

$$= DEL^j(SEL^{ij}\{*[ADID^{ij}(E^n)]\})$$

$$= *\{HOOKID^{ij}[ADID^{ij}(E^n)]\} \quad .$$

We may now proceed to generalize ADID and HOOKID in the following ways. First, we define them for a single list of superscripts $i(1), i(2), \ldots, i(k)$, which we may abbreviate as I. Second, we define them for a list of lists of indices

$$I(1) = i(1,1), i(1,2), \ldots, i(1,k_1) \quad ,$$

$$I(2) = i(2,1), i(2,2), \ldots, i(2,k_2) \quad ,$$

$$\ldots\ldots\ldots\ldots\ldots\ldots\ldots\ldots\ldots\ldots\ldots\ldots$$

$$I(a) = i(a,1), i(a,2), \ldots, i(a,k_a) \quad .$$

For the propriety of the definitions, a prior understanding is necessary with regard to the superscript lists $I(j)$. First, for each such list $I(j)$, namely

$$I(j) = i(j,1), i(j,2), \ldots, i(j,k_j) \quad ,$$

we must have that

$$1 \leq i(j,1) < i(j,2) < \ldots < i(j,k_j) \leq n \quad ,$$

where n is the adicity of the element to which the generalized ADID or HOOKID operator is to be applied. And, second, we must have that every member of any of the lists $I(1), I(2), \ldots, I(a)$ is distinct from every other member of any of the lists. This requirement is made to guarantee that no one adicity place or hook is referenced more than once by the generalized operations.

Now, with this understanding, and with the understanding that $n \geq 2$, we define the generalized ADID and HOOKID operators by induction, as indicated in the following:

$$\text{ADID}^I(E^n) = \text{ADID}^{i(1)i(2) \cdots i(k)}(E^n)$$

is the element

$$\text{ADID}^{i(1)i(2)}\{ \ldots \text{ADID}^{i(1)i(k-1)}[\text{ADID}^{i(1)i(k)}(E^n)] \ldots \} \quad .$$

And

$$\text{HOOKID}^I(E^n) = \text{HOOKID}^{i(1)i(2) \cdots i(k)}(E^n)$$

is the element

$$\text{HOOKID}^{i(1)i(2)}\{ \ldots \text{HOOKID}^{i(1)i(k-1)}[\text{HOOKID}^{i(1)i(k)}(E^n)] \ldots \} \quad .$$

Also,

$$\text{ADID}^{I(1)I(2) \cdots I(a)}(E^n)$$

is the element

$$\text{ADID}^{I(a)}\{ \ldots \text{ADID}^{I(2)}[\text{ADID}^{I(1)}(E^n)] \ldots \} \quad .$$

The most general form of HOOKID works like the most general form of ADID, except that superscripts are generally more difficult to specify, because the superscripts of the different superscript lists may overlap in magnitude. Thus, we may define

$$\text{HOOKID}^{I(1)I(2) \cdots I(a)}(E^n)$$

as the element

$$\text{HOOKID}^{I(a)'}\{ \ldots [\text{HOOKID}^{I(2)'}(\text{HOOKID}^{I(1)'}[E^n])] \ldots \} \quad ,$$

where $I(2)'$ is obtained systematically from $I(2)$ and $I(1)$, $I(3)'$ is obtained systematically from $I(3)$, $I(2)$, and $I(1)$, and so forth.

The method for obtaining these new superscript lists is this. For each list of superscripts $I(j) = i(j,1)i(j,2) \ldots i(j,k_j)$, for $1 \leq j \leq a$, and for each superscript $i(j,p)$ of $I(j)$, we define the integer $n(j,p)$ as follows: if $j = 1$, then $n(j,p) = 0$; and if $j \geq 2$, then $n(j,p)$ is the number of *all* superscripts in the lists $I(1)$, $I(2), \ldots, I(j-1)$ that are *less than* $i(j,p)$ in magnitude. Similarly, for each list of superscripts $I(j) = i(j,1)i(j,2) \ldots i(j,k_j)$, for $1 \leq j \leq a$, and for each superscript $i(j,p)$ of $I(j)$, we define the integer $m(j,p)$ as follows: if $j = 1$, then $m(j,p) = 0$; and if $j \geq 2$, then $m(j,p)$ is the number of *first* superscripts in the lists $I(1), I(2), \ldots, I(j-1)$ that are *less than* $i(j,p)$ in magnitude. (In other words, $m(j,p)$ is the number of indices in the set $\{i(1,1), i(2,1), \ldots, i(j-1,1)\}$ that are *less than* $i(j,p)$ in magnitude.) Then, for each list $I(j)$ we define the list $I(j)' = i(j,1)'i(j,2)'\ldots i(j,k_j)'$ as follows:

$$i(j,p)' = i(j,p) - n(j,p) + m(j,p) \quad .$$

The semantics for the generalized ADID and HOOKID operators is simply an extension of the semantics for $ADID^{ij}$ and $HOOKID^{ij}$, respectively. Thus, for example,

$$*[ADID^{i(1)i(2)\,\cdots\,i(k)}(E^n)] = SEL^{i(1)i(2)\,\cdots\,i(k)}[*(E^n)] \quad ;$$

and

$$*[HOOKID^{i(1)i(2)\,\cdots\,i(k)}(E^n)] =$$
$$DEL^{i(2)i(3)\,\cdots\,i(k)}\{SEL^{i(1)i(2)\,\cdots\,i(k)}[*(E^n)]\} \quad .$$

For the most general form of the ADID and HOOKID operators, the semantics is as follows. For all Enterpretations $(D,*)$,

$$*[ADID^{I(1)I(2)\,\cdots\,I(a)}(E^n)] = SEL^{I(1)I(2)\,\cdots\,I(a)}[*(E^n)] \quad .$$

For the HOOKID operator the semantics is more tedious to specify, owing to the fact that superscripts in the various lists $I(j)$ may overlap in magnitude. For each superscript list $I(j)$, let the superscript list $I(j)'$ be defined as before. And now we define, for each j with $1 \le j \le a$, the superscript list $I(j)''$ to be the list obtained from $I(j)'$ by deleting from it its *first*, and consequently its smallest, superscript while retaining all its other superscripts. Then, for all Enterpretations $(D,*)$,

$$*[HOOKID^{I(1)I(2)\,\cdots\,I(a)}(E^n)] =$$
$$DEL^{I(a)''}\{SEL^{I(a)'}[\ldots DEL^{I(2)''}(SEL^{I(2)'}\{DEL^{I(1)''}[SEL^{I(1)'}(*[E^n])]\})\ldots]\} \quad .$$

We may note here, as a generalization of an earlier point, that for all Enterpretations $(D,*)$,

$$*[HOOKID^{I(1)I(2)\,\cdots\,I(a)}(E^n)] =$$
$$*\{HOOKID^{I(1)I(2)\,\cdots\,I(a)}[ADID^{I(1)I(2)\,\cdots\,I(a)}(E^n)]\} \quad .$$

The following Propositions are stated without proof, and are easily verifiable.

Proposition 7.7: If an element E^0 is of the form $J_1^{12}(E^2)$, then for all Enterpetations $(D,*)$, $*[COMMA^0(E^0)] = *[HOOKID^{12}(E^2)]$.

Proposition 7.8: If an element E^0 is of the form $J_2{}^{12}(E^1, F^1)$, then for all Enterpretations $(D, *)$, $*[COMMA^0(E^0)] = *\{J_2{}^{12}[E^1, COMMA^1(F^1)]\} = *\{J_2{}^{23}[COMMA^1(E^1), F^1]\}$.

The following theorem is of great importance for the presentation of the the Representation Theorem of the following section of this work in terms of graphical syntax.

Theorem 7.5: For all elements of PAL E^n, with $n \geq 2$, and for all Enterpretations $(D, *)$, $*\{HOOKID^{ij}[NEG(E^n)]\} = *\{NEG[HOOKID^{ij}(E^n)]\}$. And, more generally, at the semantic level, all the generalized HOOKID operators commute in this way with the NEG operator.

Proof: We prove the theorem explicitly for a pair of superscripts i and j. Because the generalized HOOKID operators are defined inductively from HOOKID^{ij}, the general result follows from the explicitly proved result.

So, let an Enterpretation $(D, *)$ be given, and let the universal class of n-tuples over D be V^n, and let the null class of n-tuples over D be Z^n, as usual. We may first take note that $DEL^j[SEL^{ij}(Z^n)] = Z^{n-1}$. Secondly, we may show that $DEL^j[SEL^{ij}(V^n)] = V^{n-1}$ as follows. $SEL^{ij}(V^n)$ is the class of all n-tuples over D of the form

$$(d_1, d_2, \ldots, d_{i-1}, d, d_{i+1}, \ldots, d_{j-1}, d, d_{j+1}, \ldots, d_n) \quad .$$

It follows that $DEL^j[SEL^{ij}(V^n)]$ is the class of all $(n-1)$-tuples over D of the form

$$(d_1, d_2, \ldots, d_{i-1}, d, d_{i+1}, \ldots, d_{j-1}, d_{j+1}, \ldots, d_n) \quad ,$$

which is V^{n-1}.

Now we recall that for all $n \geq 0$, $\langle V^n \rangle = Z^n$ and that $\langle Z^n \rangle = V^n$. We also note that, for any element E^n with $n \geq 2$,

$$*\{HOOKID^{ij}[NEG(E^n)]\} = DEL^j\{SEL^{ij}[\langle *(E^n) \rangle]\}$$

and that

$$*\{NEG[HOOKID^{ij}(E^n)]\} = \langle DEL^j\{SEL^{ij}[*(E^n)]\} \rangle \quad .$$

Let, therefore, any element E^n with $n \geq 2$ be given. There are three cases to consider.

Case 1: Suppose $*(E^n) = V^n$. Then $*\{HOOKID^{ij}[NEG(E^n)]\}$

$$= DEL^j\{SEL^{ij}[\langle *(E^n) \rangle]\}$$

$$= DEL^j\{SEL^{ij}[\langle V^n \rangle]\}$$

$$= DEL^j\{SEL^{ij}[Z^n]\} = Z^{n-1} \quad .$$

And $*\{NEG[HOOKID^{ij}(E^n)]\} = \langle DEL^j\{SEL^{ij}[*(E^n)]\} \rangle$

$$= \langle DEL^j\{SEL^{ij}[V^n]\}\rangle$$

$$= \langle V^{n-1}\rangle = Z^{n-1} \quad .$$

Case 2: Suppose $*(E^n) = Z^n$. Then $*\{HOOKID^{ij}[NEG(E^n)]\}$

$$= DEL^j\{SEL^{ij}[\langle *(E^n)\rangle]\}$$

$$= DEL^j\{SEL^{ij}[\langle Z^n\rangle]\}$$

$$= DEL^j\{SEL^{ij}[V^n]\} = V^{n-1} \quad .$$

And $*\{NEG[HOOKID^{ij}(E^n)]\} = \langle DEL^j\{SEL^{ij}[*(E^n)]\} \rangle$

$$= \langle DEL^j\{SEL^{ij}[Z^n]\} \rangle$$

$$= \langle Z^{n-1}\rangle = V^{n-1} \quad .$$

Case 3: Suppose that $*(E^n)$ is neither V^n nor Z^n. In this case it is clear that, for all Enterpretations $(D,*)$, $*(E^n)$ and $\langle *(E^n)\rangle$ are non-intersecting classes of n-tuples over D whose union is V^n. It follows that $SEL^{ij}[*(E^n)]$ and $SEL^{ij}[\langle *(E^n)\rangle]$ are non-intersecting classes of n-tuples whose union is $SEL^{ij}(V^n)$. Now, DEL^j deletes but one, the jth, column of a matrix, leaving the other columns, including the ith column, intact. Hence, if $DEL^j\{SEL^{ij}[*(E^n)]\}$ and $DEL^j\{SEL^{ij}[\langle *(E^n)]\rangle\}$ had any $(n-1)$-tuple in common, then $SEL^{ij}[*(E^n)]$ and $SEL^{ij}[\langle *(E^n)\rangle]$ would have to have an n-tuple in common, because every n-tuple in $SEL^{ij}[*(E^n)]$ and in $SEL^{ij}[\langle *(E^n)\rangle]$ contains the same member of D in both the ith and the jth places. So, it follows that $DEL^j\{SEL^{ij}[*(E^n)]\}$ and $DEL^j\{SEL^{ij}[\langle *(E^n)\rangle]\}$ are non-intersecting classes of $(n-1)$-tuples. Moreover, the union of these two classes of $(n-1)$-tuples is clearly $DEL^j[SEL^{ij}(V^n)] = V^{n-1}$. From this it immediately follows that

$$DEL^j\{SEL^{ij}[\langle *(E^n)\rangle]\} = \langle DEL^j\{SEL^{ij}[*(E^n)]\} \rangle \quad .$$

And with this, the theorem is proved.

q.e.d.

The next operator to be introduced, PRODUCT, enables us to do something that heretofore we have not been able to do, namely to regard arrays of PAL of chorisis 2 *as if they were single elements* (that is, as arrays of chorisis 1), and to treat them as such. Through iterated application, PRODUCT enables us to treat arrays having arbitrarily large chorisis n as if they were single elements. Because PRODUCT lets us treat all arrays as single elements, it is a kind of key that opens the door to our being able to *negate* any term of PAL. Moreover, PRODUCT in concert with HOOKID allows us to introduce into PAL the ability to form generalized conjunctions. With negation and *generalized conjunction* at our disposal, the reduction thesis of this work is a short step away.

In order to introduce PRODUCT, we first define an operation PROPROD on elements E^n of PAL of adicity $n \geq 0$. PROPROD has no special interest in its own right; it is presented merely as ancillary to the definition of PRODUCT.

Definition 7.5: By definition, if $n \geq 0$, then PROPROD(E^n) is the element

$$J_2^{n+1,n+2}[\text{COMMA}^n(E^n), U^2] \quad .$$

We may note in particular that if E^0 is an element of adicity 0, then PROPROD$(E^0) = J_2^{12}[\text{COMMA}^0(E^0), U^2]$.

Proposition 7.9: For all Enterpretations $(D,*)$, and all elements E^n with $n \geq 0$,

$$*[\text{PROPROD}(E_n)] = *(E^n) \times V^1 \quad ,$$

where V^1, as usual, is the class of 1-tuples over D containing every 1-tuple over D except the null 1-tuple over D.

Proof: (Part 1) Let us first consider only the cases $n \geq 1$. In general,

$$*[\text{PROPROD}(E^n)] = *\{J_2^{n+1,n+2}[\text{COMMA}^n(E^n), U^2]\}$$
$$= SD^{n+1,n+2}\{*[\text{COMMA}^n(E^n)] \times *(U^2)\} \quad .$$

We may now take note that for all interpretations $(D,*)$, and for $n \geq 1$,

$$*[\text{COMMA}^n(E^n)] \times *(U^2)$$

is the class X^{n+3} consisting of all $(n+3)$-tuples over D of the form

$$(d_1, d_2, \ldots, d_n, d_n, b, c) \quad ,$$

with $(d_1, d_2, \ldots, d_n)$ being in $*(E^n)$ and with b and c both being members of D.

Now,

$$SD^{n+1,n+2}(X^{n+3})$$

is the class of all $(n+1)$-tuples over D of the form

$$(d_1, d_2, \ldots, d_n, c) \quad ,$$

with $(d_1, d_2, \ldots, d_n)$ being in $*(E^n)$ and with c being a member of D. But this class is $*(E^n) \times V^1$.

(Part 2) Let us now consider the case n = 0. In general,

$$*[\text{PROPROD}(E^0)] = *\{J_2{}^{12}[\text{COMMA}^0(E^0),U^2]\}$$
$$= SD^{12}\{*[\text{COMMA}^0(E^0)] \times *(U^2)\}$$
$$= DEL^{12}[\text{SEL}^{12}\{*[\text{COMMA}^0(E^0)] \times V^2\}] \quad .$$

Now, by Proposition 7.5, $*[\text{COMMA}^0(E^0)] = Z^1$ if $*(E^0) = \bot$ and $*[\text{COMMA}^0(E^0)] \neq Z^1$ if $*(E^0) = \mathsf{T}$. Now,

$$DEL^{12}[\text{SEL}^{12}(Z^1 \times V^2)] = Z^1,$$

and, if $X^1 \neq Z^1$,

$$DEL^{12}[\text{SEL}^{12}(X^1 \times V^2)] = V^1 \quad .$$

It follows that $*[\text{PROPROD}(E^0)] = Z^1$ if $*(E^0) = \bot$, and $*[\text{PROPROD}(E^0)] = V^1$ if $*(E^0) = \mathsf{T}$. But $Z^1 = \bot \times V^1$, and $V^1 = \mathsf{T} \times V^1$. Hence, in any case, $*[\text{PROPROD}(E^0)] = *(E^0) \times V^1$.

q.e.d.

It is now in terms of PROPROD that we may define PRODUCT.

Definition 7.6: For $n \geq 0$ and $m \geq 0$, let E^n and F^m be an n-adic element and an m-adic element of PAL, respectively. Then, by definition, PRODUCT(E^n,F^m) is the element

$$J_2{}^{n+1,n+m+2}[\text{PROPROD}(E^n),\text{PROPROD}(F^m)] \quad .$$

The adicity of the element PRODUCT(E^n,F^m) is clearly $n + m$, because PROPROD yields a result of adicity 1 greater than that of its argument.

Proposition 7.10: For all Enterpretations (D,*), and all elements E^n and F^m with $n \geq 0$ and $m \geq 0$, $*[\text{PRODUCT}(E^n,F^m)] = *(E^n) \times *(F^m)$.

Proof: (Part 1) We first prove the theorem for $n \geq 1$ and $m \geq 1$. In general,

$$*\{J_2{}^{n+1,n+m+2}[\text{PROPROD}(E^n),\text{PROPROD}(F^m)]\}$$
$$= SD^{n+1,n+m+2}\{*[\text{PROPROD}(E^n)] \times *[\text{PROPROD}(F^m)]\}$$
$$= DEL^{n+1,n+m+2}\{\text{SEL}^{n+1,n+m+2}[*(\text{PROPROD}(E^n)) \times *(\text{PROPROD}(F^m))]\}.$$

But, for $n \geq 1$ and $m \geq 1$, $*(\text{PROPROD}(E^n)) \times *(\text{PROPROD}(F^m))$ is the class X^{n+m+2} of all $(n + m + 2)$-tuples of the form

$$(e_1, e_2, \ldots, e_n, b, f_1, f_2, \ldots, f_m, c) \quad ,$$

with $(e_1, e_2, \ldots, e_n)$ in $*(E^n)$, $(f_1, f_2, \ldots, f_m)$ in $*(F^m)$, and both b and c members of D. Now, $DEL^{n+1,n+m+2}\{\text{SEL}^{n+1,n+m+2}[*(\text{PROPROD}(E^n)) \times *(\text{PROPROD}(F^m))]\}$ is the class of all $(n + m)$-tuples over D of the form

$$(e_1, e_2, \ldots, e_n, f_1, f_2, \ldots, f_m) \quad ,$$

with $(e_1, e_2, \ldots, e_n)$ in $*(E^n)$ and with $(f_1, f_2, \ldots, f_m)$ in $*(F^m)$. But this class is the class of $(n + m)$-tuples $*(E^n) \times *(F^m)$.

(Part 2) We now prove the theorem for $n = 0$ and $m \geq 1$. In general, $*[PRODUCT(E^0,F^m)]$

$$= *\{J_2^{1,m + 2}[PROPROD(E^0),PROPROD(F^m)]\}$$

$$= SD^{1,m + 2}\{*[PROPROD(E^0)] \times *[PROPROD(F^m)]\}$$

$$= DEL^{1,m + 2}\{SEL^{1,m + 2}[*(PROPROD(E^0)) \times *(PROPROD(F^m))]\} \ .$$

Now, if $*(E^0) = \bot$, then $*[PRODUCT(E^0,F^m)]$

$$= DEL^{1,m + 2}\{SEL^{1,m + 2}[Z^1 \times (*(F^m) \times V^1)]$$

$$= Z^m = \bot \times *(F^m) = *(E^0) \times *(F^m).$$

Now, if $*(E^0) = \mathsf{T}$, then $*[PRODUCT(E^0,F^m)]$

$$= DEL^{1,m + 2}\{SEL^{1,m + 2}[V^1 \times (*(F^m) \times V^1)]$$

$$= *(F^m) = \mathsf{T} \times *(F^m) = *(E^0) \times *(F^m).$$

(Part 3) The proof of the theorem for $n \geq 1$ and $m = 0$ is similar to the proof in Part 2.

(Part 4) Proving the theorem for $n = 0$ and $m = 0$ is straightforward, once the following facts are taken account of:

$$DEL^{12}\{SEL^{12}[Z^1 \times Z^1]\} = \bot \quad ;$$

$$DEL^{12}\{SEL^{12}[V^1 \times Z^1]\} = \bot \quad ;$$

$$DEL^{12}\{SEL^{12}[Z^1 \times V^1]\} = \bot \quad ;$$

and

$$DEL^{12}\{SEL^{12}[V^1 \times V^1]\} = \mathsf{T} \quad .$$

q.e.d.

This means that PRODUCT furnishes us with the means of regarding any array of chorisis 2 as a single element in the sense that any relation expressible as such an array is also expressible as a single element of PAL.

Before continuing with further analysis we should take note that, as is easily proved,

$$*[PROPROD(E^n)] = *[PRODUCT(E^n,U^1)] = *(E^n) \times V^1 \quad .$$

PRODUCT may now easily be generalized into KPRODUCT, an operator on any array of elements of PAL. KPRODUCT is really a collection of operators lPRODUCT, 2PRODUCT, 3PRODUCT, and so forth. The definitions are by induction.

Definition 7.7: lPRODUCT(E^n), for n ≥ 0, is the element E^n. For n ≥ 0 and m ≥ 0, 2PRODUCT(E^n,F^m) is the element PRODUCT(E^n,F^m). And, in general,

KPRODUCT(E_1, E_2, . . . , E_k)

is the element

PRODUCT[(k − 1)PRODUCT(E_1, E_2, . . . , E_{k-1}), E_k]   .

Through KPRODUCT we may regard any array of PAL as if it were an element of PAL.

With KPRODUCT at hand, we may now at last construct the NEGATION of any term of PAL. Let t be an array of PAL of chorisis k, where, of course, k ≥ 1. Then:

NEGATION(t)

is the element

NEG[KPRODUCT(t)]   .

For the sake of simplicity of notation, the NEGATION operator will henceforth in this work be written simply as NEG. If, therefore, the term t is any array of chorisis k, where k ≥ 1, the expression NEG(t) should be understood to be the element NEG[KPRODUCT(t)].

Through the KPRODUCT operators and the HOOKID operators, we may construct all the conjunctions that can be constructed in quantificational logic. That is, we can construct in PAL any conjunction involving any number of conjuncts and involving variable identifications of every possible variety. For, let $E_1^{n(1)}$, $E_2^{n(2)}$, . . . , $E_k^{n(k)}$ be k elements of PAL corresponding to the k well-formed formulae $R_1(x_1, x_2, . . . , x_{n(1)})$, $R_2(y_1, y_2, . . . , y_{n(2)})$, . . . , $Rk(z_1, z_2, . . . , z_{n(k)})$ of quantificational logic (first-order predicate logic with identity), respectively. Note carefully here that all the variables in the k formulae are understood to be distinct. Then:

KPRODUCT($E_1^{n(1)}$, $E_2^{n(2)}$, . . . , $E_k^{n(k)}$)

corresponds to the conjunction

$R_1(x_1, x_2, . . . , x_{n(1)})$ & $R_2(y_1, y_2, . . . , y_{n(2)})$ & . . . & $R_k(z_1, z_2, . . . , z_{n(k)})$

of quantificational logic. If now we want to express in PAL a relation expressed in quantificational logic by a conjunction in which variables are identified with each other, we may use the HOOKID operators, superscripted according to the variables to be identified, in order to accomplish this. The method is an obvious one.

As one example of applying it, however, let us construct in PAL the Boolean Product of two elements of the same adicity n. In quantificational logic, the Boolean Product is given by the conjunction

$$R_1(x_1, x_2, \ldots, x_n) \ \& \ R_2(x_1, x_2, \ldots, x_n) \quad ,$$

and is ordinarily called the conjunction of the two relations. We may note that the first variable of R_1 is identified with the first variable of R_2, the second variable of R_1 is identified with the second variable of R_2, and so forth, with no other identifications being made. Hence, if R_1 and R_2 correspond to the terms E_1 and E_2 of PAL, respectively, then the Boolean Product of the relations expressed by E_1 and E_2, in that order—which we can write as BOOLEPRODUCT(E_1,E_2)—is an element of PAL determined as follows.

For j with $1 \le j \le n$, let the superscript list I(j) be the two-entry list

$$j, n + j \quad .$$

Then:

BOOLEPRODUCT(E_1,E_2)

is the element

HOOKID$^{I(1)I(2) \cdots I(n)}$ [2PRODUCT(E_1,E_2)]   .

This, in turn is, of course, the element

HOOKID$^{n,n+1}$\{ . . . HOOKID$^{2,n+1}$[HOOKID$^{1,n+1}$(2PRODUCT(E_1,E_2))]\} .

It should be clear that with NEG now applying to all terms of PAL (because they may be regarded as elements), and with generalized conjunction available, we may construct all the operations of quantificational logic. For example, the disjunction

$$R_1(x_1, x_2, \ldots, x_n) \ \lor \ R_2(x_1, x_2, \ldots, x_n)$$

may be defined as

NEG\{BOOLEPRODUCT[NEG(E_1),NEG(E_2)]\}   ,

where E_1 and E_2 are both elements of adicity n that correspond to $R_1(x_1, x_2, \ldots, x_n)$ and to $R_2(x_1, x_2, \ldots, x_n)$, respectively.

NOTES

1. Kloesel, et al., 1984, pp. 372-376.

8

A REPRESENTATION THEOREM
FOR PEIRCEAN ALGEBRAIC LOGIC

Currently, the standard first-order predicate logic with identity (which will also be called "quantificational logic") serves as a kind of canonical vehicle for semeiosis. In the discussion of this section, it will be proved that, corresponding to any well-formed formula w of quantificational logic, there is a term t of PAL that is a *translation* of w, in a natural sense. The discussion provides, indeed, a translation scheme for converting well-formed formulae of quantificational logic into terms of PAL.

Let, therefore, QL be the standard first-order predicate logic with identity, but without function symbols or constants. (The exclusion of function symbols is a minor matter, because functions can be defined in terms of predicates. The exclusion of constants is also a minor matter, because constants can be eliminated in a predicate logic with identity, and also because the formalism of PAL could easily—although in opposition to the Peircean spirit of intensionalism—be altered in order to incorporate constants.) It will be proved in this section that any well-formed formula of QL is translatable into a term of PAL.

We begin by correlating, to each predicate symbol $\mathbf{R}_i^n$ of adicity n of QL a primitive term R_i^n of adicity n of PAL. To the dyadic identity relation symbol "=" we correlate the primitive term 1^2 of PAL. The term R_i^n of PAL will be called *the primitive term of PAL correlated with* the predicate symbol $\mathbf{R}_i^n$ of quantificational logic.

We are now ready for the main definition of this section.

Definition 8.1: Let w be a well-formed formula of QL that is in prenex normal form and that contains in its matrix only the propositional operators ¬ (negation) and & (conjunction). Also let w be such that it involves no "empty" quantifications, such as $(\forall x)(\exists y)Fy$, and no "redundant" quantifications, such as $(\forall y)(\exists y)Fy$. Then a term t of PAL will be said to be *the translation of w in PAL* if and only if t is constructed according to the following scheme:

(1) Let b be the matrix of w. And let b′ be the well-formed formula obtained from b by making each occurrence of a variable in b′ to be an occurrence of a distinct variable, otherwise leaving b′ exactly like b. Now b′ is

capable of being built up by successively applying the propositional operators $\neg$ and & to a finite stock of primitive well-formed formulae of quantificational logic, that is to say formulae of the form $\mathbf{R}(x_1, x_2, \ldots, x_n)$ where $\mathbf{R}$ is a predicate of adicity n and $x_1, x_2, \ldots, x_n$ are variables that are distinct from each other and from all other variables occurring in any of the formulae in the stock. More exactly, there is a sequence $b_0, b_1, \ldots, b_k$, with b_k being identical to b', such that each b_i in the sequence is either:

(a)   a primitive formula $\mathbf{R}(x_1, x_2, \ldots, x_n)$ with each variable-occurrence being an occurrence of a variable distinct from all others occurring in the formula or in any previous member of the sequence; or

(b)   the negation $\neg(b_j)$ of some previous member b_j of the sequence $(j < i)$; or

(c)   the conjunction $b_{j(1)}$ & $b_{j(2)}$ of two previous members $b_{j(1)}$, $b_{j(2)}$ of the sequence $(j(1) < i, j(2) < i, j(1) \neq j(2))$.

Now, construct the term t' of PAL as follows. Construct the sequence of terms of PAL $t_0, t_1, \ldots, t_k$, with t_k being identical to t', such that:

(a)   if b_i is a primitive formula $\mathbf{R}(x_1, x_2, \ldots, x_n)$—all of whose variables are, of course, distinct—then t_i is the primitive term R_i^n of PAL that is *correlated with* the predicate symbol $\mathbf{R}$; and

(b)   if b_i is $\neg(b_j)$ for $j < i$, then t_i is $\mathrm{NEG}(t_j)$; and

(c)   if b_i is $b_{j(1)}$ & $b_{j(2)}$, for $j(1) < i$ and $j(2) < i$, then t_i is PRODUCT $(t_{j(1)}, t_{j(2)})$—or, equivalently, $2\mathrm{PRODUCT}(t_{j(1)}, t_{j(2)})$.

(2) *Now, construct from t' a term of PAL t_b* as follows: simply apply HOOKID, appropriately superscripted, to t' in such a way as to accomplish the identifications of variables that were made distinct in the transition from b to b'. To put the procedure more exactly, note that the adicity places (hooks) of t' may be numbered to correspond with the variable-occurrences of b', and thus with the variable-occurrences of b, in a straightforward manner. That is to say, we may consider the variable-occurrences (and, indeed, also the variables) in b' to be numbered in order going from left to right, so that each such occurrence may be designated by an integer 1, 2, etc. and so that we may unambiguously refer to the jth variable-occurrence in b'. Now, because the hooks of each primitive term of PAL that occurs in t' correspond to the variable-occurrences of the primitive well-formed formula of QL with which the primitive term of PAL is correlated, it is obvious that the hooks of t' may be numbered to correspond with the variable-occurrences of b', so that a hook of t' will be numbered by the integer j if and only if that

hook corresponds to the jth variable-occurrence in b'. But, because the variable-occurrences of b' are correlated one-to-one with the variable-occurrences of b, it follows that the hooks of t' may be numbered to correspond to the variable-occurrences of b.

Now, number the *variables* in b in order of their *first* occurrence in b going from left to right. And designate by x(j) the jth variable that occurs in b *with more than 1 occurrence.* Then, for each variable x (j) in b with more than one occurrence in b, we let the superscript list I[x(j)] be the list of integers i[j(1)], i [j(2)], . . . , i[j(k_j)], with $1 \leq i[j(1)] < i[j(2)] < \ldots < i[j(k_j)]$, such that any integer i [j(m)] is one of the entries in this list if and only if the i[j(m)]th occurrence of a variable in b is an occurrence of the variable x(j). Now b contains only a finite number of variable-occurrences. Hence, if there are any variables that occur more than once in b, then there is a positive integer n such that the variables x(1), x(2), . . . , x(n) are *all* the variables that occur more than once in b. Now, if there is no variable in b that occurs more than once in b, then the term of PAL t_b is the term t', which is an element of PAL. And, if there is at least one variable in b with more than one occurrence in b, then the term of PAL t_b is the element

HOOKID$^{I[x(1)]I[x(2)] \ldots I[x(n)]}$(t')   .

(3) Now construct from t_b the term t as follows. Construct a finite sequence of terms of PAL $\alpha_0, \alpha_1, \ldots, \alpha_m$, where α_0 is t_b and α_m is the required term t, and where m is the number of quantifiers in the prefix of w, in the following manner. Consider the sequence of well formed formulae of quantificational logic $w_0, w_1, \ldots, w_m$, where w_0 is b, w_m is w, and where each entry in the sequence is obtained from the immediately preceding entry in the sequence by applying a quantifier to this preceding entry in accord with the quantifiers of the prefix of w going from right to left (from innermost quantifier to outermost quantifier).

Now, for each w_i, with $0 \leq i \leq m - 1$, in the sequence, and for each free variable x_j of w_i, assign the integer n(i,j) to the variable x_j if and only if x_j is the n(i,j)th free variable to occur in w_i *counting from left to right.* In this way, each free variable of each w_i in the sequence, for $0 \leq i \leq m - 1$, has a number assigned to it relative to i. The sequence $\alpha_0, \alpha_1, \ldots, \alpha_m$ is therefore constructed as follows. α_0 is t_b. Also, for each i, $1 \leq i \leq m$, α_i is obtained from α_{i-1} as follows. If the left-most (outermost) quantifier of w_i is

$(\exists x_j)$,

then α_i is the element

$$\text{QUANT}^{n(i-1,j)}(\alpha_{i-1}) \quad ;$$

and if the left-most (outermost) quantifier of w_i is

$$(\forall x_j) \quad ,$$

then α_i is the element

$$\text{NEG}\{\text{QUANT}^{n(i-1,j)}[\text{NEG}(\alpha_{i-1})]\} \quad .$$

The required term t, the translation of w in PAL, is the term α_m.

This ends the definition.

Now, let the notion of an interpretation of QL be defined in the standard way, as a pair $M = (D,F)$, where D is a non-empty set and F is a function mapping each n-adic predicate symbol $\mathbf{R}_i^n$ of QL to a subset of D^n (perhaps the null set $\emptyset$). In a well-known way, M determines a function f from all the well-formed formulae of QL containing n free variables, for $n \geq 1$, to subsets of D^n, such that if w is a well-formed formula of QL containing n distinct free variables, for $n \geq 1$, then f(w) is the subset of D^n containing every member of D^n that "satisfies" w, where the notion that a member of D^n "satisfies" w can be defined in a straightforward way from the standard Tarskian notion of the satisfaction of well-formed formulae by sequences of members of D. *Intuitively*, the idea of "satisfaction" is this. The n free variables of w are considered to be numbered in the order of their first occurrence in w, going from left to right; so that, for example, in $\mathbf{R}_i^5(x,x,y,x,z)$, x is the first free variable, y is the second free variable and z is the third free variable. Then, w is considered to be "satisfied" by a member $(d_1, d_2, \ldots, d_n)$ of D^n provided that, when for all i with $1 \leq i \leq n$, d_i is considered as being the value of the ith free variable of w, the result can be appropriately considered, in light of M, to be a true assertion. In a well-known way also, M determines a notion of truth (truth-in-M) for all well-formed formulae of QL not containing any free variables (the closed sentences of QL), such that for any such well-formed formula w, w is true-in-M or w is false-in-M. Moreover, the function f and the notion of truth behave in the following ways.

(a) If w is a primitive well-formed formula $\mathbf{R}_i^n(x_1, x_2, \ldots, x_n)$ of QL, where all the variables $x_1, x_2, \ldots, x_n$ are *distinct*, then $f(w) = F(\mathbf{R}_i^n)$.

(b) $f(\neg w)$ is the complement in D^n of $f(w)$. In particular, if $f(w) = D^n$, then $f(\neg w) = \emptyset$, and if $f(w) = \emptyset$, then $f(\neg w) = D^n$.

(c) If w_1 and w_2 both have at least one free variable and the two well-formed formulae have no free variables in common, then $f(w_1$ & $w_2) = f(w_1) \times f(w_2)$, where $f(w_1) \times f(w_2)$ is defined to be the concatenation of every member of $f(w_1)$ with every member of $f(w_2)$, it being understood that if either $f(w_1) = \emptyset$ or $f(w_2) = \emptyset$ then $f(w_1) \times f(w_2) = \emptyset$. If w_1 is a closed sentence of QL and w_2 has at least one free variable, then $f(w_1$ & $w_2) = f(w_2)$ if w_1 is true-in-M, and $f(w_1$ & $w_2) = \emptyset$ if w_1 is false-in-M. If w_1 has at least one free variable and w_2 is a closed sentence of QL, then $f(w_1$ & $w_2)$ = w_1 if w_2 is true-in-M, and $f(w_1$ & $w_2) = \emptyset$ if w_2 is false-in-M.

(d) If w has n distinct free variables, with $n \geq 2$; and if the variable x is the jth free variable of w, when the n free variables of w are numbered in the order of their first occurrence in w going from left to right, then $f[(\exists x)w]$ is the subset of D^{n-1} consisting of every member of D^{n-1} that is obtainable from a member of $f(w)$ by striking out its jth entry.

(e) If w has only the single free variable x, then $(\exists x)w$ is true-in-M if and only if $f(w) \neq \emptyset$, and $(\exists x)w$ is false-in-M if and only if $f(w) = \emptyset$.

(f) Suppose that $n \geq 2$ and that w' is such that all n of its occurrences of free variables are occurrences of *distinct* variables; and suppose that w differs from w' *only in that*, in the $i(1)^{th}$, $i(2)^{th}, \ldots,$ and $i(j)^{th}$ positions where w' has j occurrences of distinct free variables, w has j occurrences of *the same* free variable; *then* $f(w)$ is the subset of D^{n-j+1} consisting of every member of D^{n-j+1} that is obtainable from any member of $f(w')$ that contains *the same* member of D as entry in its $i(1)^{th}$, $i(2)^{th}, \ldots,$ and $i(j)^{th}$ places by *deleting* from it its $i(2)^{th}$, $i(3)^{th}, \ldots,$ and $i(j)^{th}$ entries; if there is no member of $f(w')$ that contains the same member of D in its $i(1)^{th}$, $i(2)^{th}, \ldots,$ and $i(j)^{th}$ places, then $f(w) = \emptyset$.

If w is a closed sentence of QL, then the expression $f(w)$ has no meaning. In Definition 8.2 and Definition 8.3, however, we proceed to define in context the expression $f(w)$ for w a closed sentence of QL. In this way, the meaning of $f(w)$ is extended to cases in which w contains no free variables. When w does contain free variables, the expression $f(w)$ and any expression of which $f(w)$ is a part are to be understood as having their usual meanings.

Definition 8.2: If w is a closed sentence of QL, then the expression $f(w) \neq \emptyset$ means that w is true-in-M, and the expression $f(w) = \emptyset$ means that w is false-in-M. If w contains at least one free variable, then the two expressions have their usual meanings.

If both w_1 and w_2 are closed sentences of QL, then it is clear that $f(w_1 \& w_2) = \emptyset$ if and only if $f(w_1) = \emptyset$ or $f(w_2) = \emptyset$, and that $f(w_1 \& w_2) \neq \emptyset$ if and only if $f(w_1) \neq \emptyset$ and $f(w_2) \neq \emptyset$.

Definition 8.3: Let D be any set not containing either of the truth values T, $\perp$; and let M = (D,F) be any interpretation of QL with domain D. Also, let (D,*) be any Enterpretation of PAL. Also, let w be a well-formed formula of QL and t be a term of PAL. And let f be the function determined by F, as described immediately above. Then we will say that f(w) *coincides with* *(t) if and only if: *Either* (A) the number of free variables of w = the adicity of t = n, where $n \geq 1$, *and* either $f(w) \neq \emptyset$ and $f(w) = *(t)$ or $f(w) = \emptyset$ and $*(t) = (Z^n)_D$, the class of n-tuples containing only the null n-tuple over D; *Or else* (B) the number of free variables of w = the adicity of t = 0, *and* either $f(w) \neq \emptyset$ (that is, w is true-in-M) and $*(t) = \mathsf{T}$ or $f(w) = \emptyset$ (that is, w is false-in- M) and $*(t) = \perp$. The assertion that f(w) coincides with *(t) will be written as:

$$f(w) \approx *(t) \quad .$$

Definition 8.4: Let D be any set not containing either of the truth values T, $\perp$; and let M = (D,F) be any interpretation of QL with domain D. Then the Enterpretation of PAL *corresponding to M* is the Enterpretation $(D,*_{fD})$ of PAL whose Enterpretation function $*_{fD}$ maps terms of PAL to classes of n-tuples over D such that, for every predicate symbol $\mathbf{R}_i^n$ of QL, if R_i^n is the primitive term of PAL correlated with $\mathbf{R}_i^n$, we have that:

$$*_{fD}(R_i^n) = F(\mathbf{R}_i^n)$$

if $F(\mathbf{R}_i^n) \neq \emptyset$; and

$$*_{fD}(R_i^n) = (Z^n)_D$$

if $F(\mathbf{R}_i^n) = \emptyset$, where $\emptyset$ is the null set and where $(Z^n)_D$ is the class of n-tuples containing only the null n-tuple over D.

It should be explicitly noted in connection with this definition that D^n and the universal class $(V^n)_D$ of n-tuples over D are simply the same thing.

Several propositions are now in order. In connection with them too it needs to be kept in mind that $D^n = (V^n)_D$.

Proposition 8.1: Let $\mathbf{R}_i^n(x_1, x_2, \ldots, x_n)$ be a primitive well-formed formula of QL, and let all the variables $x_1, x_2, \ldots, x_n$ be distinct. Then, if R_i^n is the primitive term of PAL corresponding to the predicate symbol $\mathbf{R}_i^n$,

$$f[\mathbf{R}_i^n(x_1, x_2, \ldots, x_n)] \approx *_{fD}(R_i^n) \quad .$$

Proof: In light of clause (a) concerning the function f determined by F,

$$f[\mathbf{R}_i^n(x_1, x_2, \ldots, x_n)] = F(\mathbf{R}_i^n).$$

Now, if $F(\mathbf{R}_i^n) \neq \emptyset$, then—by the definition of $*_{fD}$—$*_{fD}(R_i^n) = F(\mathbf{R}_i^n)$, so that

$$f[\mathbf{R}_i^n(x_1, x_2, \ldots, x_n)] = *_{fD}(R_i^n) \quad ,$$

and the result follows. But, if $F(\mathbf{R}_i^n) = \emptyset$, then—by the definition of $*_{fD}$—$*_{fD}(R_i^n) = Z^n$, and again the result follows.

q.e.d.

Proposition 8.2: Let D be a set not containing either of the truth values $\mathsf{T}, \bot$. Let an interpretation $M = (D,F)$ be given, and let f be the function determined by F as described above. Furthermore, let $(D,*)$ be any Enterpretation of PAL with domain D; and let w be any well-formed formula of QL with n distinct free variables, and let t be a term of PAL such that $f(w) \approx *(t)$. Then

$$f(\neg w) \approx *[NEG(t)] \quad .$$

Proof: There are five cases to consider. *Case 1:* $n \geq 1$ and $f(w) = D^n$. Then: $*(t) = D^n = (V^n)_D$. It follows that $f(\neg w) = \emptyset$, and that $*[NEG(t)] = (Z^n)_D$, and the result follows. *Case 2:* $n \geq 1$ and $f(w) = \emptyset$. Then: $*(t) = (Z^n)_D$. It follows that $f(\neg w) = D^n$, and that $*[NEG(t)] = (V^n)_D = D^n$, and the result follows. *Case 3:* $n \geq 1$ and $f(w) \neq D^n$ and $f(w) \neq \emptyset$. In this case it is clear that $f(\neg w) = *[NEG(t)]$, so that the result follows. *Case 4:* $n = 0$, so that w has no free variables, and $f(w) = \emptyset$. Then $*(t) = \bot$. It follows that $f(\neg w) \neq \emptyset$ and that $*[NEG(t)] = \mathsf{T}$, so that the result follows. *Case 5:* $n = 0$, so that w has no free variables, and $f(w) \neq \emptyset$. Then $*(t) = \mathsf{T}$. It follows that $f(\neg w) = \emptyset$ and that $*[NEG(t)] = \bot$, so that the result follows.

q.e.d.

Proposition 8.3: Let D be a set not containing either of the truth values $\mathsf{T}, \bot$. Let an interpretation $M = (D,F)$ be given, and let f be the function determined by F as described above. Furthermore, let $(D,*)$ be any Enterpretation of PAL with domain D. Now, if w_1 and w_2 are any two well-formed formulae of QL that have no free variables in common; and if t_1 and t_2 are two terms of PAL such that $f(w_1) \approx *(t_1)$ and $f(w_2) \approx *(t_2)$, then

$$f(w_1 \,\&\, w_2) \approx *[\text{PRODUCT}(t_1, t_2)] \quad .$$

Proof: There are four cases to consider. *Case 1:* Both w_1 and w_2 are closed sentences of QL. Then the number of distinct free variables of w_1, of w_2, and of $w_1 \,\&\, w_2$, as well as the adicity of $\text{PRODUCT}(t_1, t_2)$, are all 0. Now, $f(w_1 \,\&\, w_2) \neq \emptyset$ if and only if both $f(w_1) \neq \emptyset$ and $f(w_2) \neq \emptyset$, which in turn is the case if and only if both $*(t_1) = \mathsf{T}$ and $*(t_2) = \mathsf{T}$. Hence, $f(w_1 \,\&\, w_2)$ $\neq \emptyset$ if and only if $*[\text{PRODUCT}(t_1, t_2)] = \mathsf{T}$, so that the result follows. *Case 2:* w_1 is a closed sentence of QL and w_2 contains at least one free variable. Now, there are two subcases to consider. First, assume that $f(w_1) \neq \emptyset$; then $f(w_1 \,\&\, w_2) = f(w_2)$, and $*(t_1) = \mathsf{T}$. It follows that $*[\text{PRODUCT}(t_1, t_2)] = \mathsf{T}$ $\times *(t_2) = *(t_2)$. Because, by hypothesis, $f(w_2) \approx *(t_2)$, the result follows. Second, assume that $f(w_1) = \emptyset$; then $f(w_1 \,\&\, w_2) = \emptyset$, and $*(t_1) = \perp$. It follows that $*[\text{PRODUCT}(t_1, t_2)] = \perp \times *(t_2) = (Z^n)_D$, where n is the adicity of t_2. The result then follows immediately. *Case 3:* w_1 contains at least one free variable and w_2 is a closed sentence of QL. The argument for this case proceeds just as with Case 2, *mutatis mutandis. Case 4:* Both w_1 and w_2 contain at least one free variable. Now there are two subcases to consider. First, assume that $f(w_1) \neq \emptyset$ and that $f(w_2) \neq \emptyset$. Then, $f(w_1)$ $= *(t_1)$ and $f(w_2) = *(t_2)$, so that $f(w_1 \,\&\, w_2) = f(w_1) \times f(w_2) = *(t_1) \times *(t_2)$ $= *[\text{PRODUCT}(t_1, t_2)]$, and the result follows. Second, assume that either $f(w_1) = \emptyset$ or $f(w_2) = \emptyset$. Then, $f(w_1 \,\&\, w_2) = \emptyset$, and either $*(t_1) =$ $(Z^n)_D$ or $*(t_2) = (Z^m)_D$, where n is the adicity of t_1 and m is the adicity of t_2. It follows that $*[\text{PRODUCT}(t_1, t_2)] = (Z^{n+m})_D$, so that the result follows.

q.e.d.

Proposition 8.4: Let D be a set not containing either of the truth values T, $\perp$. Let an interpretation $M = (D, F)$ be given, and let f be the function determined by F as described above. Furthermore, let $(D, *)$ be any Enterpretation of PAL with domain D. Now, if w is a well-formed formula of QL that has n distinct free variables, with $n \geq 2$; and if the variable x is the jth free variable of w, when the n free variables of w are numbered in the order of their first occurrence in w going from left to right; and if t is a term of PAL such that $f(w) \approx *(t)$, then

$$f[(\exists x)w] \approx *[\text{QUANT}^j(t)] \quad .$$

Proof: The result follows immediately from clause (d) concerning the function f and from the definition of the QUANT operator.

Proposition 8.5: Let D be a set not containing either of the truth values $\top$, $\bot$. Let an interpretation M = (D,F) be given, and let f be the function determined by F as described above. Furthermore, let (D,*) be any Enterpretation of PAL with domain D. Now, if w is a well-formed formula of QL that has only the single free variable x; and if t is a term of PAL such that $f(w) \approx *(t)$, then

$$f[(\exists x)w] \approx *[QUANT^1(t)] \quad .$$

Proof: $f[(\exists x)w] \neq \emptyset$ (that is to say, $(\exists x)w$ is true-in-M) if and only if $f(w) \neq \emptyset$, and $f[(\exists x)w] = \emptyset$ (that is to say, $(\exists x)w$ is false-in-M) if and only if $f(w) = \emptyset$. But, because $f(w) \approx *(t)$, it follows that $f(w) = \emptyset$ if and only if $*(t) = Z^1$. Thus, $f[(\exists x)w] = \emptyset$ if and only if $*[QUANT^1(t)] = \bot$. Also, obviously, both the number of distinct free variables of $(\exists x)w$ and the adicity of $QUANT^1(t)$ are 0. The result then follows.

Proposition 8.6: Let D be a set not containing either of the truth values $\top$, $\bot$. Let an interpretation M = (D,F) be given, and let f be the function determined by F as described above. Furthermore, let (D,*) be any Enterpretation of PAL with domain D. Now, if w is a well-formed formula of QL that has n distinct free variables, with $n \geq 1$; and if the variable x is the jth free variable of w, when the n free variables of w are numbered in the order of their first occurrence in w going from left to right; and if t is a term of PAL such that $f(w) \approx *(t)$, then

$$f[(\exists x)w] \approx *[QUANT^j(t)] \quad .$$

Proof: From Proposition 8.4 and Proposition 8.5.

Proposition 8.7: Let D be a set not containing either of the truth values $\top$, $\bot$. Let an interpretation M = (D,F) be given, and let f be the function determined by F as described above. Furthermore, let (D,*) be any Enterpretation of PAL with domain D. Now, suppose that $n \geq 2$ and that w′ is such that all n of its occurrences of free variables are occurrences of *distinct* variables; and suppose that w differs from w′ *only in that,* in the $i(1)^{th}$, $i(2)^{th}$, . . . , and $i(j)^{th}$ positions where w′ has j occurrences of distinct free variables, w has j occurrences of *the same* free variable. And suppose that t′ and t are terms of PAL such that $f(w') \approx *(t')$ and $f(w) \approx *(t)$. Then:

$$f(w) \approx *[HOOKID^{i(1)i(2) \cdots i(j)}(t')] \quad .$$

Proof: The result follows immediately from clause (f) concerning the function f and from the definition of the HOOKID operator.

The main theorem of this section now follows.

Theorem 8.1: (Representation Theorem for PAL) Let w be a well-formed formula of QL of the sort specified in Definition 8.1, and let t be the translation of w in PAL. Also, let M = (D,F) be any interpretation of QL, and let $(D,*_{fD})$ be the corresponding Enterpretation of PAL. Then:

$$f(w) \approx *_{fD}(t).$$

Proof: We first cite several general facts, which are simply particular applications of the Propositions proved above.

(a) (from Proposition 8.2) If w is any well-formed formula of QL and t is any term of PAL and $f(w) \approx *_{fD}(t)$, then

$$f(\neg w) \approx *_{fD}[NEG(t)] \qquad .$$

(b) (from Proposition 8.3) If w_1 and w_2 are any two well-formed formulae of QL that have no free variables in common; and if t_1 and t_2 are two terms of PAL such that $f(w_1) \approx *_{fD}(t_1)$ and $f(w_2) \approx *_{fD}(t_2)$, then

$$f(w_1 \And w_2) \approx *_{fD}[PRODUCT(t_1,t_2)] \qquad .$$

(c) (from Proposition 8.6) If w is a well-formed formula of QL that has n distinct free variables, with $n \geq 1$; and if the variable x is the jth free variable of w, when the n free variables of w are numbered in the order of their first occurrence in w going from left to right; and if t is a term of PAL such that $f(w) \approx *_{fD}(t)$, then

$$f[(\exists x)w] \approx *_{fD}[QUANT^j(t)] \qquad .$$

(d) (from Proposition 8.7) Suppose that $n \geq 2$ and that w′ is such that all n of its occurrences of free variables are occurrences of *distinct* variables; and suppose that w differs from w′ *only in that*, in the $i(1)^{th}$, $i(2)^{th}$, . . . , and $i(j)^{th}$ positions where w′ has j occurrences of distinct free variables, w has j occurrences of *the same* free variable. And suppose that t′ and t are terms of PAL such that $f(w') \approx *_{fD}(t')$ and $f(w) \approx *_{fD}(t)$. Then:

$$f(w) \approx *_{fD}[HOOKID^{i(1)i(2) \cdots i(j)}(t')] \qquad .$$

Now we begin the body of the proof of the theorem.

First, consider the sequence $b_0, b_1, \ldots, b_k$ of well-formed formulae of QL and the sequence $t_0, t_1, \ldots, t_k$ of terms of PAL as defined in Definition 8.1. It may be proved straightforwardly that for each i, with $0 \leq i \leq k$,

$$f(b_i) \approx *_{fD}(t_i) \qquad .$$

This follows from Proposition 8.1, Proposition 8.2 (or general fact (a) above), and Proposition 8.3 (or general fact (b) above), and induction. Because b_k is b' and t_k is t', it is clear that

$$f(b') \approx *_{fD}(t') \quad .$$

Now, consider the well-formed formula b of QL and the term t_b of PAL. From Proposition 8.7 (or general fact (d) above), and the definition of the HOOKID operator, together with a straightforward induction, it follows that

$$f(b) \approx *_{fD}(t_b) \quad .$$

Now, consider the sequence $w_0, w_1, \ldots, w_m$ of well-formed formulae of QL, and the sequence $\alpha_0, \alpha_1, \ldots, \alpha_m$ of terms of PAL. It may be straightforwardly proved that for all i, with $0 \leq i \leq m$,

$$f(w_i) \approx *_{fD}(\alpha_i) \quad .$$

This follows from the fact that w_0 is b, the fact that α_0 is t_b, Proposition 8.6 (or general fact (c) above), the fact that the universal quantifier $(\forall x)$ is definable in terms of the existential quantifier and negation as $\neg(\exists x)\neg$, and induction. The method is obvious and needs no special discussion.

Because, now, w_m is w and α_m is t, we thus have that

$$f(w) \approx *_{fD}(t) \quad .$$

q.e.d.

Corollary 8.1.1: Any well-formed formula w of QL may be translated into a term t of PAL such that, with f and $*_{fD}$ defined as in the theorem,

$$f(w) \approx *_{fD}(t) \quad .$$

Proof: For we may algorithmically transform any well-formed formula of QL into a logically equivalent well-formed formula in prenex normal form, having no redundant or empty quantifiers and having only the propositional operators $\neg$ and & in its matrix.

q.e.d.

NOTES

1. Mendelson, 1987, pp. 46ff.

9

HYPOSTATIC ABSTRACTION
AND THE REDUCTION THEOREM

In one sense, the representation theorem itself shows that, when triadic relations are included in the resources of PAL, these resources are adequate for expressing all relations. The sense in question, of course, requires that the idea of "expressing relations" be defined in terms of the translatability of well-formed formulae of quantificational logic into terms of PAL. In this section, the idea of "expressing relations" will be understood to be defined—as previous sections of this work have defined it—in terms of the semantics for PAL. In this sense also, as we shall see, when triadic relations are included in the resources of PAL, PAL is adequate for expressing all relations. Indeed, it may be shown that all relations may be expressed as constructions from relations exclusively of adicities 1, 2, and 3. The reduction theorems of this section explicate precisely the sense in which this is so.

For the purpose of proving these theorems, only one Peircean idea remains to be introduced: the idea of hypostatic abstraction. We may begin our consideration of hypostatic abstraction by considering an example from Peirce. The example is that of the triadic relation

x_1 gives x_2 to x_3 ,

or, as Peirce sometimes specifies it,

x_1 is a giver of x_2 to x_3 .

Abstracting hypostatically on this relation consists of asserting that there is at least one entity of a special sort of entities: namely, instances or examples or acts of giving. We might also call these entities "givings" or instances of the obtaining of the triadic relation of giving. Abstraction also involves replacing the assertion that

d_1 gives d_2 to d_3

by the assertion that there is a particular "giving" such that d_1 has a certain dyadic relation to it (the relation, namely, of being *donor* with regard to it), d_2 has a second dyadic relation to it (the relation of being *donated* with regard to it), and d_3 has a third dyadic relation to it (the relation of being *recipient* with regard to it).

In quantificational logic, this hypostatic abstraction would be represented by replacing the primitive well-formed formula

$G(x_1, x_2, x_3)$

with the well-formed formula

$(\exists y) [\mathbf{G}(y) \ \& \ I_1(x_1, y) \ \& \ I_2(x_2, y) \ \& \ I_3(x_3, y)]$,

where $\mathbf{G}(y)$ stands for the monadic relation "y is a giving," $I_1(x_1, y)$ stands for the dyadic relation "x_1 is donor with regard to y," $I_2(x_2, y)$ stands for the dyadic relation "x_2 is donated with regard to y," and $I_3(x_3, y)$ stands for the dyadic relation "x_3 is recipient with regard to y."

More generally, what is done in one typical sort of hypostatic abstraction is to replace a relation of adicity n with a certain kind of combination of one monadic relation and n dyadic relations in which a single existential quantification is involved. Thus, by this sort of hypostatic abstraction, the well-formed formula of quantificational logic

$R(x_1, x_2, \ldots, x_n)$,

with all the variables $x_1, x_2, \ldots, x_n$ distinct, would be replaced by the formula

$(\exists y) [\mathbf{R}(y) \ \& \ I_1(x_1, y) \ \& \ I_2(x_2, y) \ \& \ \ldots \ \& \ I_n(x_n, y)]$.

Note that it is not quite right to say that in this sort of hypostatic abstraction, a relation $\Re$ is replaced by an entity, a single entity. (That, of course, *can* happen: when it is provable that $(\exists! y)\mathbf{R}(y)$.) It would be more accurate to say that a relation $\Re$ is replaced by a collection of entities, all of which are of the same sort, namely, instances or examples of the obtaining of $\Re$.

The underlying idea of the reduction thesis of this work is that hypostatic abstraction should be universally available, that is to say, that hypostatic abstraction should be applicable to any relation of any adicity $n \geq 1$. In terms of PAL this means that any relation that may be expressed by a primitive term R^n of PAL may also be expressed by

$\text{QUANT}^1 \{\text{HOOKID}^{1,3,5,\ldots,2n+1}[(n+1)\text{PRODUCT}(\mathbf{R}^1, I_1{}^2, I_2{}^2, \ldots, I_n{}^2)]\}$,

where $\mathbf{R}^1$ stands for the monadic relation "being *an obtaining* of the relation that R^n expresses,"; $I_1{}^2$ stands for the dyadic relation "being the occupant of the *first* adicity place (hook) of _____"; $I_2{}^2$ stands for the dyadic relation "being the occupant of the *second* adicity place (hook) of _____"; and so forth.

From the surface-appearance of the representation of hypostatic abstraction in the formalism of quantificational logic, it might seem that by hypostatic abstraction we accomplish some sort of reduction of relations of adicity 3 and higher to relations purely dyadic and monadic. This appearance might seduce some philosophers—particularly, perhaps, those who may be impressed with Arthur Skidmore's attack on Peirce's reduction thesis (Skidmore, 1971)—into doubting the reduction thesis of this work. But this apparent absence of the triadic is deceptive, for hypostatic abstraction involves *in every case* QUANT, HOOKID, and PRODUCT, all of which are definable in PAL only through the teridentity relation. This general point is true even in cases of hypostatically abstracting on dyadic and monadic relations. For example, hypostatic abstraction applied to a monadic relation expressed by a primitive term P^1 of PAL yields a replacement of P^1 by the element

$$\text{QUANT}^1\{\text{HOOKID}^{1,3}[2\text{PRODUCT}(\mathbf{P}^1, \text{I}_1{}^2)]\} \quad .$$

Hypostatic abstraction, therefore, always involves an appeal to the triadic. And for this reason all attempts to refute the reduction thesis of this work by arguing analogously to Skidmore's argument against Peirce's reduction thesis must fail.

The fundamental idea of the reduction thesis of this work is that all relations of adicity higher than 3 may be reduced to relations of adicities 1, 2, and 3 by means of hypostatic abstraction. In order to show exactly what this means and to prove the thesis correct, we shall need to present hypostatic abstraction from the point of view of logical semantics. And in order to present the semantics for hypostatic abstraction, a few preliminary informal remarks are necessary for the purpose of motivating the formal constructions that will follow.

Given an Enterpretation (D,*) of PAL, let R^n be a primitive term of adicity n of PAL. Then $*(R^n)$ is some class of n-tuples over D. Now, in applying hypostatic abstraction, we are in effect asserting that there are entities that in general must be considered to be *new*, that is, beyond the entities in D. We are asserting that there are, namely, the various *obtainings* (concrete instances of the obtaining) of the class of n-tuples $*(R^n)$ expressed by R^n on (D,*). Now, aside from philosophical niceties, each n-tuple

$$(d_1, d_2, \ldots, d_n)$$

in $*(R^n)$ "is", we might say, a unique "obtaining" of the class of n-tuples expressed by R^n on (D,*), namely that obtaining in which d_1 is the occupant of the first adicity place in the obtaining, d_2 is the occupant of the second adicity place in the obtaining, and so forth. Given (D,*), therefore, $*(R^n)$ contains *all* the obtainings of the class of n-tuples expressed by R^n on (D,*).

If $*(R^n) = (Z^n)_D$, then there are no obtainings of the class of n-tuples expressed by R^n on $(D,*)$.

It follows from the foregoing that an account of the sort of hypostatic abstraction under consideration must involve, at the level of semantics, constructions whereby, for a given Interpretation ι, whenever a relation expressed on ι by a primitive term R^n is dealt with by hypostatic abstraction, the domain D_w, for each w in W, is *augmented by new members* equivalent in number to the number of n-tuples in $[\iota(R^n)](w)$, with each new member understood to correspond with exactly one of the n-tuples in $[\iota(R^n)](w)$. One way to do this would be to augment D_w with a set of entities E_w of equivalent cardinality with that of $[\iota(R^n)](w)$, and to have a one-to-one correspondence at hand between E_w and $[\iota(R^n)](w)$. A simpler and more elegant way, however, is simply to allow the members *of* $[\iota(R^n)](w)$ *themselves*, considered as individuals in their own right rather than as n-tuples of individuals in D_w, to be added to D_w. This simpler method for augmenting D_w will be the one presented in Theorem 9.1. The more complicated method is in effect used in Theorem 9.2.

The foregoing ideas motivate the following definition as well as its intensional analogue in Definition 9.2. In it, and also in Definition 9.2, the device is employed of *adding new terms* to PAL. This device is chosen merely for the purpose of simplifying the exposition of the basic ideas, and should not be thought to imply the production of a new language beyond PAL. For it should be obvious that the same ideas could be captured formally—though laboriously and in a manner not very intuitively natural—by *reserving* certain primitive terms of PAL for the special purposes that are served by the "new" terms, which are described in Definition 9.1 and in Definition 9.2 as *added* to PAL.

Definition 9.1: Let R^n be any primitive term of PAL. And let any Enterpretation $(D,*)$ be given. Then, *the augmentation of $(D,*)$ by hypostatic abstraction with respect to the term R^n is the Enterpretation $(D^+,*^+)$, where $D^+ = D \cup *(R^n)$, and where $*^+$ is the Enterpretation function mapping terms of PAL together with n + 1 new primitive terms that are added to PAL, namely

$$\mathbf{R}^1, I_1{}^2, I_2{}^2, \ldots, I_n{}^2 \quad ,$$

to classes, and to finite sequences of classes, of n-tuples over D^+, in accord with the following specifications:

(a) *+ maps all terms of PAL other than terms involving the new terms $\mathbf{R}^1$, $I_1{}^2$, $I_2{}^2$, . . . , $I_n{}^2$ to the *same* class, or finite sequences of classes, of n-tuples as * does;

(b) $^{*+}(\mathbf{R}^1) = X^1$, the class of 1-tuples (e) *over D^+* such that a 1-tuple (e) over D^+ is a member of X^1 if and only if e is an n-tuple *over D* that is a member of $*(\mathbf{R}^n)$; if $*(\mathbf{R}^n) = (Z^n)_D$, then $^{*+}(\mathbf{R}^1) = (Z^1)_{D+}$.

(c) for all i, with $1 \leq i \leq n$, $^{*+}(I_i{}^2) = X_i{}^2$, the class of all 2-tuples (d,e) *over D^+* such that a 2-tuple (d,e) over D^+ is a member of $X_i{}^2$ if and only if (e) is a 1-tuple of X^1 (so that e is an n-tuple *over D* that is a member of $*(\mathbf{R}^n)$) *and* d is the ith entry of e; if $*(\mathbf{R}^n) = (Z^n)_D$, then for all i with $1 \leq i \leq n$, $^{*+}(I_i{}^2) = (Z^2)_{D+}$.

We are now ready to prove the central theorem involved in the reduction thesis of this work.

Theorem 9.1 (Extensional Reduction Theorem for PAL): Any class X^n of n-tuples, for $n \geq 1$, over any set D not containing either of the truth values $\top$, $\bot$, is constructible from classes of n-tuples of adicities 1, 2, and 3 exclusively, in the following sense. Let such a class X^n be given. And let a primitive term R^n, of adicity n, of PAL be given. Moreover, let (D,*) be any Enterpretation of PAL such that $*(R^n) = X^n$. And, let (D+,*+) be the augmentation of (D,*) by hypostatic abstraction with respect to the term R^n, with the primitive terms $\mathbf{R}^1$, $I_1{}^2$, $I_2{}^2$, . . . , I_2^n being as specified in the definition of (D+,*+). Then the class of n-tuples $X^n = *(\mathbf{R}^n)$ expressed on (D,*) by R^n is also expressed on (D+,*+) by

$$\text{QUANT}^1\{\text{HOOKID}^{1,3,5,\ldots,2n+1}[(n+1)\text{PRODUCT}(\mathbf{R}^1, I_1{}^2, I_2{}^2, \ldots, I_n{}^2)]\} .$$

That is to say, $X^n = *(\mathbf{R}^n) =$

$$^{*+}[\text{QUANT}^1\{\text{HOOKID}^{1,3,5,\ldots,2n+1}[(n+1)\text{PRODUCT}(\mathbf{R}^1, I_1{}^2, I_2{}^2, \ldots, I_n{}^2)]\}] .$$

Proof: If X^n is $(Z^n)_D$, then the theorem is obviously true. If X^n is not $(Z^n)_D$, then we proceed as follows. The crucial class of n-tuples in question is obviously

$$^{*+}[\text{QUANT}^1\{\text{HOOKID}^{1,3,5,\ldots,2n+1}[(n+1)\text{PRODUCT}(\mathbf{R}^1, I_1{}^2, I_2{}^2, \ldots, I_n{}^2)]\}] .$$

By virtue of the qualities of any Enterpretation function, this class of n-tuples is given by

$$\text{DEL}^1[\text{DEL}^{3,5,\ldots,2n+1}\{\text{SEL}^{1,3,\ldots,2n+1}[^{*+}(\mathbf{R}^1) \times {}^{*+}(I_1{}^2) \times \ldots \times {}^{*+}(I_n{}^2)]\}] .$$

Now, the innermost Cartesian Product

$$*^+(\mathbf{R}^1) \times *^+(I_1{}^2) \times \ldots \times *^+(I_n{}^2) =$$
$$X^1 \times X_1{}^2 \times X_2{}^2 \times \ldots \times X_n{}^2 \quad ,$$

is the class of all $(2n+1)$-tuples over D^+ of the form

$$(e, d_{i(1)}, e_{i(1)}, d_{i(2)}, e_{i(2)}, \ldots, d_{i(n)}, e_{i(n)}) \quad ,$$

where (e) is a 1-tuple of X^1, and for all j, with $1 \le j \le n$, $(d_{i(j)}, e_{i(j)})$ is a 2-tuple of $X_j{}^2$. So, this innermost Cartesian Product is the class of all $(2n + 1)$-tuples over D^+ of the form

$$((d_1, d_2, \ldots, d_n), d_{i(1)}, e_{i(1)}, d_{i(2)}, e_{i(2)}, \ldots, d_{i(n)}, e_{i(n)}) \quad ,$$

where $(d_1, d_2, \ldots, d_n)$ is an n-tuple of $*(R^n)$ and where each $e_{i(j)}$ is a member of X^1, and each $d_{i(j)}$ is the jth entry of $e_{i(j)}$.

Now, applying to this class of $(2n + 1)$-tuples the operator $SEL^{1,3,\ldots,2n+1}$ yields the class of all $(2n + 1)$-tuples of the form

$$((d_1, d_2, \ldots, d_n), d_1, (d_1, d_2, \ldots, d_n), d_2, (d_1, d_2, \ldots, d_n) \ldots$$
$$d_n, (d_1, d_2, \ldots, d_n)) \quad ,$$

where $(d_1, d_2, \ldots, d_n)$ is an n-tuple of $*(R^n)$.

Applying to this class of $(2n + 1)$-tuples the operator $DEL^{3,5,\ldots,2n+1}$ yields the class of all $(n + 1)$-tuples of the form

$$((d_1, d_2, \ldots, d_n), d_1, d_2, \ldots, d_n) \quad ,$$

where $(d_1, d_2, \ldots, d_n)$ is an n-tuple of $*(R^n)$.

Finally, applying to this class of $(n + 1)$-tuples the operator DEL^1 yields the class of all n-tuples of the form

$$(d_1, d_2, \ldots, d_n) \quad ,$$

where $(d_1, d_2, \ldots, d_n)$ is an n-tuple of $*(R^n)$. But this class of n-tuples just *is* the class of n-tuples $*(R^n)$.

q.e.d.

The following theorem, with minor differences, was proved by Herzberger in "Peirce's Remarkable Theorem" (Herzberger, 1981).

Theorem 9.2: (Herzberger's Theorem) Let X^n be any class of n-tuples, for $n \ge 1$, over any domain D of Enterpretation; and let the cardinality of D be at least as great as the cardinality of X^n. Then, there is a term t^n of adicity n of PAL that is constructible entirely from terms of PAL of adicities 1, 2, and/or 3, such that for some Enterpretation (D,*), $*(t^n) =$

X^n. This means that, if $n > 3$, X^n is reducible to classes of n-tuples of adicities 1, 2, and/or 3.

Proof: If X^n is $(Z^n)_D$, the theorem is obviously true. If X^n is not $(Z^n)_D$, then we proceed as follows. Because the cardinality of D is at least as great as the cardinality of X^n, there exists a one-to-one correspondence f from X^n to some subset of D. This one-to-one correspondence f provides a unique member of D as a representative for each n-tuple of X^n.

Now, let R^n be a primitive term of adicity n of PAL.

We may now define, by using f, what are in effect correlates of the primitive terms $\mathbf{R}^1$, I_1^2, I_2^2, . . . , I_n^2 that appear in the definition of augmentation and in Theorem 9.1. That is to say, we have the primitive terms P^1, R_1^2, R_2^2, . . . , R_n^2 of PAL. And the term t^n will be constructed from these $n + 1$ terms.

We first define the class of 1-tuples X^1 over D and n classes of 2-tuples X_1^2, X_2^2, . . . , X_n^2 over D as follows. Let X^1 be the class of all 1-tuples (e) over D, such that for some n-tuple over D $(d_1, d_2, \ldots, d_n)$ in X^n, $f[(d_1, d_2, \ldots, d_n)] = e$. And for i such that $1 \leq i \leq n$, let X_i^2 be the class of all 2-tuples (d,e) over D such that for some n-tuple $(d_1, d_2, \ldots, d_n)$ in X^n, we have both that $f[(d_1, d_2, \ldots, d_n)] = e$ and that $d = d_i$, the ith entry in $(d_1, d_2, \ldots, d_n)$.

Now, let (D,*) be such that $*(R^n) = X^n$, $*(P^1) = X^1$ and, for all i with $1 \leq i \leq n$, $*(R_i^2) = X_i^2$. Then, the required term t^n of PAL is

$$\text{QUANT}^1\{\text{HOOKID}^{1,3,5,\ldots,2n+1}[(n+1)\text{PRODUCT}(P^1, R_1^2, R_2^2, \ldots, R_n^2)]\}].$$

For, by an argument that is correlated line for line to the proof of Theorem 9.1 in an obvious way, it follows that

$$*(t^n) = X^n \quad .$$

That is to say, if X^n is $(Z^n)_D$, then the theorem is obviously true. If X^n is not $(Z^n)_D$, then we proceed as follows. The crucial class of n-tuples in question is obviously

$$*[\text{QUANT}^1\{\text{HOOKID}^{1,3,5,\ldots,2n+1}[(n+1)\text{PRODUCT}(P^1, R_1^2, R_2^2, \ldots, R_n^2)]\}].$$

In virtue of the qualities of any Enterpretation function, this class of n-tuples is given by

$$\text{DEL}^1[\text{DEL}^{3,5,\ldots,2n+1}\{\text{SEL}^{1,3,\ldots,2n+1}[*(P^1) \times *(R_1^2) \times \ldots \times *(R_n^2)]\}].$$

Now, the innermost Cartesian Product

$(P^1) \times {}^*(R_1{}^2) \times \ldots \times {}^*(R_n{}^2) =$

$X^1 \times X_1{}^2 \times X_2{}^2 \times \ldots \times X_n{}^2$,

is the class of all $(2n + 1)$-tuples over D^+ of the form

$(e, d_{i(1)}, e_{i(1)}, d_{i(2)}, e_{i(2)}, \ldots, d_{i(n)}, e_{i(n)})$,

where e is such that for some $(d_1, d_2, \ldots, d_n)$ in X^n, $f[(d_1, d_2, \ldots, d_n)] = e$, and where for all j, with $1 \leq j \leq n$, $e_{i(j)}$ is such that for some $(d_1, d_2, \ldots, d_n)$ in X^n, $f[(d_1, d_2, \ldots, d_n)] = e_{i(j)}$, and $d_{i(j)} = d_j$, the jth entry in $(d_1, d_2, \ldots, d_n)$.

Now, applying to this class of $(2n + 1)$-tuples the operator $SEL^{1,3, \ldots, 2n+1}$ yields the class of all $(2n + 1)$-tuples of the form

$(e, d_1, e, d_2, e, \ldots, d_n, e)$,

where e is such that for some $(d_1, d_2, \ldots, d_n)$ in X^n, $f[(d_1, d_2, \ldots, d_n)] = e$, and where for all j, with $1 \leq j \leq n$, d_j is the jth entry of $(d_1, d_2, \ldots, d_n)$.

Applying to this class of $(2n + 1)$-tuples the operator $DEL^{3,5, \ldots 2n+1}$ yields the class of all $(n + 1)$-tuples of the form

$(e, d_1, d_2, \ldots, d_n)$,

where e is such that for some $(d_1, d_2, \ldots, d_n)$ in X^n, $f[(d_1, d_2, \ldots, d_n)] = e$, and where for all j, with $1 \leq j \leq n$, d_j is the jth entry of $(d_1, d_2, \ldots, d_n)$.

Finally, applying to this class of $(n + 1)$-tuples the operator DEL^1 yields the class of all n-tuples of the form

$(d_1, d_2, \ldots, d_n)$,

where $(d_1, d_2, \ldots, d_n)$ is in X^n. But this class of n-tuples just *is* the class of n-tuples X^n.

q.e.d.

Corollary 9.2.1: Theorem 9.2 holds for all infinite domains.

Proof: All infinite domains are "sufficiently large" in the sense of Theorem 9.2 because, as Herzberger notes in proving his result, there is a theorem of Cantor's to the effect that, for any given finite integer n, any infinite set has the same cardinality as the set of *all* its n-tuples.

q.e.d.

A bit of commentary is now in order on the significance of the foregoing proof of Herzberger's Theorem. Deriving this result by going *through* Theorem 9.2, as has been done here, provides a reason to think that the correct Peircean account of reduction to the triadic really *should* contain the Herzbergerian limitation on its generality to domains *sufficiently large*. For Theorem 9.2 is simply one way of capturing the effect of hypostatic abstraction in connection with the reduction thesis, because hypostatic abstraction always introduces new entities (the *obtainings* of relations) onto the scene.

We now turn to the intensional analogues of the extensional ideas so far presented in this section.

Definition 9.2: Let R^n be any primitive term of PAL. And let any Interpretation ι be given. Then, *the augmentation of ι by hypostatic abstraction with respect to the term R^n* is the Interpretation ι^+, described as follows. First, let the model structure $M = (W,D)$ be augmented to produce the model structure $M^+ = (W,D^+)$ such that, for each w in W, $D_w^+ = D_w \cup [\iota(R^n)](w)$. Then ι^+ is the Interpretation by which, for every w in W, terms of PAL together with n + 1 new primitive terms that are added to PAL, namely

$$R^1, I_1^2, I_2^2, \ldots, I_n^2 \quad ,$$

are mapped to relations (relations-simpliciter) and finite sequences of relations (relations-simpliciter) in accord with the following specifications:

(a) ι^+ maps all terms of PAL other than terms involving the new terms $R^1, I_1^2, I_2^2, \ldots, I^n_2$ to the *same* relation, or finite sequence of relations, as ι does;

(b) $\iota^+(R^1)$ is such that for all w in W, $[\iota^+(R^1)](w)$ is the class of 1-tuples (e) *over* D_w^+ such that a 1-tuple (e) over D_w^+ is a member of $[\iota^+(R^1)](w)$ if and only if e is an n-tuple *over* D_w that is a member of $[\iota(R^n)](w)$; if $[\iota(R^n)](w) = (Z^n)_{Dw}$, then $[\iota^+(R^1)](w) = (Z^1)_{Dw+}$.

(c) for all i, with $1 \leq i \leq n$, $\iota^+(I_i^2)$ is such that for all w in W, $[\iota^+(I_i^2)](w)$ is the class of all 2-tuples (d,e) *over* D_w^+ such that a 2-tuple (d,e) over D_w^+ is a member of $[\iota^+(I_i^2)](w)$ if and only if (e) is a 1-tuple of $[\iota^+(R^1)](w)$ (so that e is an n-tuple *over* D_w that is a member of $[\iota(R^n)](w)$) *and* d is the ith entry of e; if $[\iota(R^n)](w) = (Z^n)_{Dw}$, then for all i with $1 \leq i \leq n$, we have that $[\iota^+(I_i^2)](w) = (Z^2)_{Dw+}$.

Theorem 9.3 (Intensional Reduction Theorem for PAL): Any relation $\mathfrak{R}$, of adicity $n \geq 1$, is constructible from relation of adicities 1, 2, and 3 exclusively, in the following sense. Let such a relation $\mathfrak{R}$ be given. And let a primitive term R^n, of adicity n, of PAL be given. Then there is an Interpretation ι

of PAL such that $\iota(R^n) = \mathfrak{R}$, and such that ι satisfies the following condition. Let ι^+ be the augmentation of ι by hypostatic abstraction with respect to the term R^n, with the primitive terms $\mathbf{R}^1, I_1{}^2, I_2{}^2, \ldots, I_n{}^2$ being as specified in the definition of ι^+. Then the relation $\mathfrak{R} = \iota(R^n)$ expressed on ι by R^n is also expressed on ι^+ by

$$\text{QUANT}^1\{\text{HOOKID}^{1,3,5,\ldots,2n+1}[(n+1)\text{PRODUCT}(\mathbf{R}^1, I_1{}^2, I_2{}^2, \ldots, I_n{}^2)]\}.$$

That is to say, $\mathfrak{R} = \iota(R^n) =$

$$\iota^+[\text{QUANT}^1\{\text{HOOKID}^{1,3,5,\ldots,2n+1}[(n+1)\text{PRODUCT}(\mathbf{R}^1, I_1{}^2, I_2{}^2, \ldots, I_n{}^2)]\}] \ .$$

Proof: Let the element E^n of PAL be the element

$$\text{QUANT}^1\{\text{HOOKID}^{1,3,5,\ldots,2n+1}[(n+1)\text{PRODUCT}(\mathbf{R}^1, I_1{}^2, I_2{}^2, \ldots, I_n{}^2)]\}.$$

Now, as we recall from Section 4 of this work, because ι and ι^+ are Interpretations of PAL, it is the case that for each w in W, $(D_w, *_{\iota w})$ and $(D_{w+}, *_{\iota w+})$ are Enterpretations of PAL. For every w in W, $*_{\iota w}(R^n) = X_w{}^n$, where $X_w{}^n$ is a class of n-tuples over D_w. Moreover, for every w in W, $(D_{w+}, *_{\iota w+})$ is the augmentation of $(D_w, *_{\iota w})$ by hypostatic abstraction with respect to the term R^n. Hence, from Theorem 9.1 it follows that for every w in W,

$$*_{\iota w+}(E^n) = X_w{}^n = *_{\iota w}(R^n) \qquad .$$

It follows that for all w in W, $[\iota^+(E^n)](w) = \mathfrak{R}(w)$, and thus that $\iota^+(E^n) = \mathfrak{R}$.

q.e.d.

Theorem 9.4 (Intensional Herzberger Theorem): Let $\mathfrak{R}$ be any relation of adicity $n \geq 1$ such that, for all w in W, the cardinality of D_w is at least as great as the cardinality of $\mathfrak{R}(w)$. Then, there is a term t^n of adicity n of PAL that is constructible entirely from terms of PAL of adicities 1, 2, and/or 3, such that for some Interpretation ι, $\iota(t^n) = \mathfrak{R}$. This means that, if $n > 3$, $\mathfrak{R}$ is reducible to relations of adicities 1, 2, and/or 3.

Proof: Because n is the adicity of the relation $\mathfrak{R}$, it follows that for each w in W, $\mathfrak{R}(w) = X_w{}^n$, where $X_w{}^n$ is a class of n-tuples over D_w. Now, from the hypothesis it follows that for each w in W, there is a one-to-one correspondence f_w from $X_w{}^n$ to some subset of D_w. Then, for each w in W, define the class $X_w{}^1$ of 1-tuples over D_w, and the n classes $X_{1w}{}^2, X_{2w}{}^2, \ldots, X_{nw}{}^2$ of 2-tuples over D_w analogously to the definitions of the class X^1 of 1-tuples over D, and the n classes $X_1{}^2, X_2{}^2, \ldots, X_n{}^2$ of 2-tuples over D, respectively, that appear in Theorem 9.2. That is to say, let $X_w{}^1$ be the class of all 1-tuples

(e) over D_w, such that for some n-tuple over D_w $(d_1, d_2, \ldots, d_n)$ in X_w^n, $f_w[(d_1, d_2, \ldots, d_n)] = e$. And for i such that $1 \le i \le n$, let X_{iw}^2 be the class of all 2-tuples (d,e) over D_w such that for some n-tuple $(d_1, d_2, \ldots, d_n)$ in X_w^n, we have both that $f_w[(d_1, d_2, \ldots, d_n)] = e$ and that $d = d_i$, the ith entry in $(d_1, d_2, \ldots, d_n)$.

Now, we have the terms $P^1, R_1^2, R_2^2, \ldots, R_n^2$ of PAL. And we let the required term t^n of PAL be

$$\text{QUANT}^1\{\text{HOOKID}^{1,3,5,\ldots,2n+1}[(n+1)\text{PRODUCT}(P^1, R_1^2, R_2^2, \ldots, R_n^2)]\}.$$

And we also let the Interpretation ι be such that for all w in W, $[\iota(R^n)](w) = X_w^n$, $[\iota(P^1)](w) = X_w^1$, and, for all i with $1 \le i \le n$, $[\iota(R_i^2)](w) = X_{iw}^2$.

Now, as we recall from Section 4 of this work, for all w in W, $(D_w, *_{\iota w})$ is an Enterpretation for PAL. Hence, it follows from Theorem 9.2 that for each w in W, $*_w(t^n) = X_w^n = \Re(w)$. And therefore $\iota(t^n) = \Re$.

q.e.d.

Corollary 9.4.1: Theorem 9.4 holds if, for all w in W, D_w is infinite.

Proof: Obvious in light of Corollary 9.2.1.

q.e.d.

The form of hypostatic abstraction developed in this section of this work and used to prove its reduction results seems to be the simplest form of hypostatic abstraction usable in this way. It is based, as we have seen, on the idea of replacing the primitive well-formed formula

$$R(x_1, x_2, \ldots, x_n) \quad ,$$

with all the variables $x_1, x_2, \ldots, x_n$ distinct, by the formula

$$(\exists y)[\mathbf{R}(y) \mathbin{\&} I_1(x_1,y) \mathbin{\&} I_2(x_2,y) \mathbin{\&} \ldots \mathbin{\&} I_n(x_n,y)] \quad ,$$

where $\mathbf{R}$ and the I_j are understood in a certain fashion.

This form of hypostatic abstraction is not, however, the only form; nor is it the only form that is usable to prove the reduction of all relations to the triadic, dyadic, and monadic. Other forms would work just as well, though some of them would involve more complexity, including more complicated augmentations of domains. In light of the developments of this section, it is easy enough to see how, for example, to prove reduction results by using a form of hypostatic abstraction that is based on replacing

$$R(x_1, x_2, \ldots, x_n) \quad ,$$

with all the variables $x_1, x_2, \ldots, x_n$ distinct, by the formula

$$(\exists y)\, [\mathbf{R}(y)\ \&\ I_1(x_1,y,x_2)\ \&\ I_2(x_2,y,x_3)\ \&\ \ldots\ \&\ I_{n-1}(x_{n-1},y,x_n)]\quad .$$

A more complicated form of hypostatic abstraction is based on replacing

$$R(x_1, x_2, \ldots, x_n)$$

by the formula

$$(\exists y_1)\ \ldots\ (\exists y_{n-1})\{[\mathbf{R}_1(y_1)\ \&\ \ldots\ \&\ \mathbf{R}_{n-1}(y_{n-1})]\ \&$$

$$[I_1(x_1,y_1,x_2)\ \&\ I_2(x_2,y_2,x_3)\ \&\ \ldots\ \&\ I_{n-1}(x_{n-1},y_{n-1},x_n)]\}\quad ,$$

where the $\mathbf{R}_j$ and the I_j are understood in a certain fashion. This form, too, is usable to prove reduction results, although its complexity is considerably greater than that of the form developed in this section. A full analysis of various forms of hypostatic abstraction and their use for proving reduction results must be the task of another work.

10

THIRDNESS AND THE CONSISTENCY
OF THE REDUCTION THESIS OF THIS WORK
WITH OTHER RESULTS IN LOGIC

The purpose of this section of this work is to discuss the consistency of the results of this work with actual and potential reductions of all relations to relations that are purely of adicity ≤ 2. For the sake of having at hand some convenient terminology, let us begin by agreeing to call non-degenerate triadicity "Thirdness." Whether Thirdness in this sense is similar to what Peirce himself understood by his metaphysical category of Thirdness is an issue that must be reserved for discussion in another work. Whatever its affiliation with Peirce's theory of categories, Thirdness in the sense of non-degenerate triadicity is the property enjoyed by the teridentity relation denoted by 1^3, as well as by any other non-degenerate triadic relation. Let us also say, by way of extending our terminology, that Thirdness is "involved" in anything that is dependent in a certain way upon any non-degenerate triadic relation. To be a little more exact, let us say that Thirdness is involved in any operation or procedure, for example a constructional operation or a definitional procedure for obtaining relations from other relations, such that, if the operation or procedure were formalized in PAL, its definition would have to presuppose the availability of at least one non-degenerate triadic relation. In this sense, Thirdness may be involved, for example, in the operations and definitions of logical and mathematical systems.

In order to acquire skill at identifying operations and procedures that involve Thirdness in this sense, we must keep in mind principally the negative parts of the reduction thesis of this work, as they are presented in Sections 5 and 6, as well as the contrast between what is available in PAL prior to, and what is available in PAL posterior to, the introduction of teridentity and non-degenerate triadic relations in general.

It should be obvious that a given reduction of all relations to those purely dyadic, or to those purely monadic and dyadic, is not automatically as such inconsistent with the reduction thesis of this work. Such a reduction is inconsistent with this reduction thesis only if it does *not* involve Thirdness in the sense just defined. Reductions that do involve Thirdness in this sense are not only not, as such, inconsistent with the reduction thesis of this work:

their results may also even be implied by the reduction thesis of this work. Every case must be considered individually. It should, however, come as no surprise that, if a given process of reduction already involves Thirdness, then in virtue of that involvement the process may be sufficiently "powerful" to allow for the reduction of all relations to relations exclusively of adicities ≤ 2.

Naturally enough, the question arises whether or not there may be constructional procedures for relations that are procedures *not formalizable in PAL*. This question will be addressed at the end of the present section. For now, let us merely remark that if a procedure or operation is not formalizable in PAL, then it is also not formalizable in a first-order quantificational language, because—as we saw in Theorem 8.1—any sentence of such a language can be translated in a natural way into PAL. This point brings us to consider two famous historical reductions of relations (in the extensional sense) to the dyadic: that of Leopold Löwenheim (1915) and that of W. V. O. Quine (1966a). Because both these reductions can be formulated in a first-order quantificational language, we need not deal with the question posed above in order to show that neither of these reductions contradicts the reduction thesis of this work.

We shall, however, first make even more explicit than heretofore certain particulars about Thirdness. Let us assume that our model structure M = (W,D) is such that for at least one w in W, D_w contains more than 1 member. Call this assumption A. Then, on the assumption that A, various previous results of this work may here be recapitulated in the slightly recast forms of Propositions 10.1–10.7. In view of Theorem 5.3 and Corollary 5.3.2, the following Proposition may be asserted without special further proof.

Proposition 10.1: Given A, any set of procedures formalizable in PAL that allows the construction of a relation of odd adicity from a set of relations all of which are of even adicity is a set of procedures that involves Thirdness. Thus, likewise involving Thirdness is any set of procedures formalizable in PAL that allows the construction of any relation of odd adicity from a set of exclusively dyadic relations.

In view of Theorem 5.4, the following Proposition may be asserted without special further proof.

Proposition 10.2: Given A, any set of procedures formalizable in PAL that allows the reduction of a non-degenerate dyadic relation to a set of exclusively monadic relations is a set of procedures that involves Thirdness.

In view of Theorem 5.5, the following Proposition may be asserted without special further proof.

Proposition 10.3: Given A, any set of procedures formalizable in PAL that allows the reduction of a non-degenerate triadic relation to a set of exclusively monadic and/or dyadic relations is a set of procedures that involves Thirdness.

In view of the Corollary 5.5.1 we can also assert without special further proof the following Proposition.

Proposition 10.4: Given A, any set of procedures formalizable in PAL that allows the reduction of a non-degenerate relation of adicity ≥ 3 to a set of exclusively monadic and/or dyadic relations is a set of procedures that involves Thirdness.

Now, in light of this proposition and Theorem 6.4, we can assert:

Proposition 10.5: Given A, any set of procedures formalizable in PAL that allows for (a) the reduction of the dyadic identity relation ID^2 to a set of exclusively monadic relations; or (b) the reduction of the triadic identity relation (teridentity) ID^3 to a set of exclusively monadic and/or dyadic relations; or (c) the reduction of the n-adic identity relation ID^n, for $n \geq 3$ to a set of exclusively monadic and/or dyadic relations, is a set of procedures that involves Thirdness.

Considering also Theorem 6.4, together with the foregoing, we can assert:

Proposition 10.6: Given A, any set of procedures formalizable in PAL that allows for the reduction of *all* relations of any *given* adicity $n \geq 3$ to a set of relations of exclusively monadic and/or dyadic relations is a set of procedures that involves Thirdness.

Considering Theorem 6.5 together with the foregoing, we can assert:

Proposition 10.7: Given A, any set of procedures formalizable in PAL that allows for (a) the reduction of the negation of the dyadic identity relation ID^2 to a set of exclusively monadic relations; or (b) the reduction of the negation of the triadic identity relation (teridentity) ID^3 to a set of exclusively monadic and/or dyadic relations; or (c) the reduction of the negation of any n-adic identity relation ID^n, for $n \geq 3$, to a set of exclusively monadic and/or dyadic relations, is a set of procedures that involves Thirdness.

In light of these propositions, we may identify the use of the following procedures in defining a method of construction of relations from relations as procedures that will yield a method of construction that involves Thirdness: (1) any convention, rule of construction, or rule for the formation of well-formed formulae that allows for the equivalent of what in quantificational logic is identifying free variables; for such a convention or rule will allow one to construct a relation of odd adicity from a set of relations of exclusively even adicity; (2) the "Streichung" operation of Bernays, because obviously it enables one to construct a relation of odd adicity from a set of relations of exclusively even adicity; (3) the formation of Boolean Products, such as those given in quantificational logic by, for example, $F(x)$ & $G(x)$, because forming Boolean Products involves identifying free variables (and indeed similarly for Boolean Sums and Boolean Differences); (4) the "Triple-Junction" operation of A. B. Kempe, because it enables one to construct a single triadic relation from a set of three dyadic relations; (5) quantification, because it enables one to construct an odd-adic relation from an even-adic relation.

We are now ready to consider the reductions to the dyadic of Leopold Löwenheim and the reduction to the dyadic of W. V. O. Quine.

Theorem 6 of Leopold Löwenheim's 1915 paper, translated as "On Possibilities in the Calculus of Relatives," says that "Every relative equation . . . is equivalent to a binary one." Ignoring subtleties, this means that in Löwenheim's system all relations of adicity ≥ 3 are reducible to a set of dyadic relations alone. Thus Löwenheim's theorem may appear to contradict the negative part of the reduction thesis of this work.

Upon examination, however, the appearance evaporates, because Thirdness can be seen to be involved in the structure of Löwenheim's apparatus for constructing relations from relations. Taken as available at the outset of the paper, for example, are the Boolean Sum and the Boolean Product. These in turn, as Quine's introductory essay in the van Heijenoort volume indicates,[1] may be thought by Löwenheim to be derivable through definitions such as, for example,

$$(a + b)_{ij} = (a)_{ij} + (b)_{ij}   ;$$

but, if so, then they rest on the prior capacity to identify free variables, which in Löwenheim's system of notation appear as the indices i,j,k,l. In any case, Löwenheim's system incorporates Thirdness in its methods of construction from the beginning, so that his reduction to the dyadic does not, as such, conflict with the reduction thesis of this work.

In "Reduction to a Dyadic Predicate," Quine invents, for any interpreted theory θ formulated in quantificational logic an interpreted theory θ' formulated in quantificational logic and containing a single dyadic predicate F; the domain of θ' is the domain of θ augmented by the set of all (unordered) pairs over the domain of θ; moreover, as Quine shows, all the formulae of θ can be systematically translated into formulae of θ'. Thus Quine has achieved a reduction to the dyadic of all relations expressible in terms of quantificational logic. But Quine's methods for constructing relations from relations involve Thirdness throughout. These methods are formulated by using devices like quantification and the identification of free variables. Because Quine's methods involve Thirdness at the outset, Quine's result as such is not inconsistent with the reduction thesis of this work. (In Ketner [1989], Quine's reduction is examined in light of the idea that the very concept of an ordered pair used by Quine involves Thirdness.)

It is now time to ask a more general question, a question not merely about actual, historical reductions to the dyadic, but also about possible reductions to the dyadic. The question is, will *any* set of constructive procedures that permits the wholesale reduction of relations to sets of exclusively monadic and/or dyadic relations be a set of procedures that involves Thirdness in the sense of this section? And this question returns us to the question whether all possible constructive procedures are formalizable in PAL. Could we, that is to say, remove the words "formalizable in PAL" from Propositions 10.1–10.7? In order to begin to answer this question we have to ask what a constructive procedure that could not be formalized in PAL would be like. It could not, as we have seen, be formalized in a first-order quantificational language. Would it, then, be formalizable in a second-order language or some yet higher-order language? If so, then I would contend that the procedure would still be formalizable in PAL. Although the topic of the use of PAL for second-order and higher-order logical purposes is outside the scope of this work, I would contend that, by virtue of its incorporating hypostatic abstraction, PAL is adequate for expressing quantification over relations, relations of relations, and so on.[2] If, however, an alleged "procedure" of relational construction or reduction is not formalizable in *any-order* language, then the question arises whether the alleged "procedure" is really a *procedure* at all. These (admittedly sketchy) thoughts prompt the following Thesis:

Thesis: All procedures of relational construction are formalizable in PAL.

Strictly speaking, of course, this Thesis does not admit of proof, because it involves an informal, intuitive notion of "a procedure of relational construction." (In respect of its containing such an informal notion, it is analogous to Church's thesis that the informal notion of "effective procedure" is adequately encoded in the exact concept of Turing computability.) Despite this unsusceptibility to proof, the Thesis does nevertheless, as we have seen, admit of heuristic arguments in its favor. And, if it should be true, then we could remove the words "formalizable in PAL" from Propositions 10.1–10.7, on the grounds that they are superfluous. We could also be sure, in general and prior to any particular investigations, that when *any* universal "reduction to the purely dyadic" is accomplished, it will involve Thirdness in the sense of this section.

NOTES

1. van Heijenoort, 1966, pp. 228-232.
2. Readers who may be interested in PAL's possible usefulness with regard to higher-order logic might consult Menzel, 1986.

11

TWO SYSTEMS OF GRAPHICAL SYNTAX
FOR PEIRCEAN ALGEBRAIC LOGIC

PAL is designed specifically to accord as closely as possible with the system of Existential Graphs that Peirce developed in the late 1890s.[1] In this section of this work, two systems of graphical syntax for PAL will be presented. Each is, however, only a minor variant of the other. On the evidence of their appearance, these systems seem to bear a close resemblance to Peirce's existential graphs. Of course, the exact relation each of the systems has to Peirce's existential graphs is a matter that must be determined by ongoing scholarship. Even if Peirce scholars should succeed in locating details in which the graphical realizations of PAL do not match Peirce's existential graphs, it should still be clear that there is a close enough resemblance between these graphical expressions and Peirce's historical system of existential graphs to make these expressions potentially useful to the Peirce scholar who wishes to attain an exact understanding of Peirce's graphs.

The main problem in matching PAL (or indeed any other algebraic or quantificational system of logic), whose notation is linear, with a graphical syntax, whose notation is 2-dimensional, is to correlate in the two systems matters of *order*. Because graphs are drawn on a two-dimensional manifold, it is clear that, unless graphs are somehow ordered in their parts, they do not correlate with the *terms* of PAL as such, but rather at most only with *assemblies of elements* of PAL. There are, however, a number of ways of ordering graphs so that, as so ordered, they correlate with *arrays*. The method presented in this section is simply to label parts of graphs with numerals that indicate a given order. Both Roman and Arabic numerals are used. Roman numerals are used to order the separate connected pieces of graphs, which correspond to the separate elements of arrays of PAL. Arabic numerals are used to order hooks or adicity places in the separate connected pieces of graphs. Let us, therefore, proceed to explicate several of the main features of PAL in terms of the two systems of graphical syntax. The fundamental goal of the graphical syntax for PAL is to represent pictorially both the primitive terms of PAL and the operations of PAL whereby elements and arrays of the most general kind are built up. Let us begin

with the primitive terms. Each primitive term is understood to stand for a
relation of an adicity ≥ 1 when it is Interpreted. Now we may pictorially represent a relation with its n hooks or adicity places in either one of the following two ways. (Of course, there are also other ways of drawing
relations.) In the first way, we may draw a relation as a spot on a surface
and represent its hooks or adicity places as *lines* radiating out from the spot
in the manner of a child's drawing of the sun and its rays. In the second
way, we may draw a relation as a spot on a surface and represent its hooks
or adicity places as *holes* punctured at even intervals around its edges. (A
third way might be to draw the relation as a spot containing little fishhooks
attached to it around its circumference.) These two ways of conceiving of
drawing relations are the bases of the two systems of graphical syntax now
to be introduced.

Thus in the first system of graphical syntax the primitive terms of PAL are
drawn as spots with lines radiating out from them; and in the second system
of graphical syntax the primitive terms of PAL are drawn as spots with holes
punctured around their edges. For example, in the first system, the primitive term R^5 would be drawn as in Figure 1.

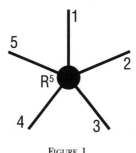

FIGURE 1

And, in the second graphical system, R^5 would be drawn as in Figure 2.

FIGURE 2

Obviously, to draw a spot of the second graphical system in complete detail,
so as to be able to see its full structure, we would need to draw it in *magnification*. In magnification we would draw the primitive term R^5 as in Figure 3.

It is to be noted that in both systems of graphical representation, the
hooks or adicity places are numbered in clockwise order (looking down on

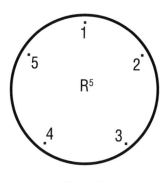

the page), starting with an adicity place in some pre-determined reference direction. In the graphs of this section, this reference direction will be understood to be directly *up* toward the top of the page. In more complicated cases, a graph must be drawn on a torus of genus 1 or greater; and in such cases a reference direction must be defined at each point of the torus in question. For tori whose genus is not very great, graphs may often still be drawn in the plane by using some sort of planar representation of a tunnel bridge.

Of special interest in both systems of graphical syntax are the *identity spots*, spots for the primitive terms 1^2, 1^3, 1^4, etc. Such spots might, of course, be represented in graphical syntax by ordinary spots labelled appropriately, just as for any other primitive terms. More conveniently, however, they may be indicated in both graphical systems by *special spots* distinguishable from all other spots by their appearance. In the first system of graphical syntax, identity spots of all adicities ≥ 2 will be represented as *points* from which radiate the appropriate number of lines to indicate hooks. In the second system of graphical syntax, identity spots of all adicities ≥ 2 will be represented as *especially small spots*, equal in size to each other, no matter what their adicity, but smaller than all other spots. Thus, the term 1^3 that denotes the teridentity relation ID^3 would be drawn in the first system of graphical syntax as in Figure 4 and in the second system of graphical syntax, magnified, as in Figure 5, where the spot of teridentity is shown in proportion to an ordinary, and thus an ordinary-*sized*, spot, say the spot for R^5. The numbering of the hooks of the teridentity spot is unimportant, though it does no harm to number them in accord with the general conventions.

The junction operations $J_1{}^{ij}$ and $J_2{}^{ij}$ may be represented in the first system of graphical syntax by connecting or joining two hooks or adicity places

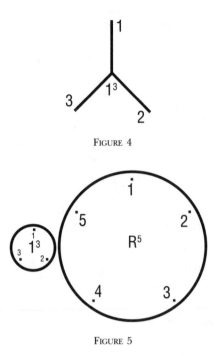

FIGURE 4

FIGURE 5

with a line drawn between them; in the case of $J_1{}^{ij}$, the hooks thus joined will be in the same connected piece of a graph (Figure 5). In the case of $J_2{}^{ij}$, the hooks thus joined will be in two separate connected pieces of a graph. For example, in the first system of graphical syntax, $J_1{}^{23}(R^4)$ would be represented by connecting hook 2 and hook 3 of Figure 6 to produce Figure 7. Note here that the unconnected hooks (let us call them "free hooks") are renumbered in an obvious fashion so as to match the ordering of the adicity places of $J_1{}^{23}(R^4)$.

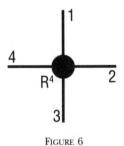

FIGURE 6

$J_2{}^{ij}$ works in a fashion similar to $J_1{}^{ij}$, except that the connecting line is drawn between two separate connected pieces of the graph. Thus, in the

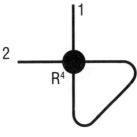

FIGURE 7

first graphical system $J_2^{25}(R^2,S^3)$, for example, would be drawn by connecting hook number 2 of the graph representing R^2 and hook number 3 of the graph representing S^3. This would take us from Figure 8 to Figure 9. Notice here too that the free hooks are renumbered in an obvious fashion so as to accord with the order of the adicity places of $J_2^{25}(R^2,S^3)$.

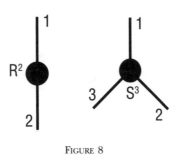

FIGURE 8

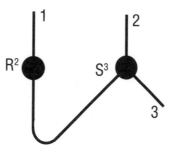

FIGURE 9

In the second system of graphical syntax, all junction operations are represented by means of $Join_2$ operations that always involve at least one identity spot. $Join_2$ operations with identity spots are represented by letting two spots, one of them an identity spot, be "directly joined" at the appropriate hooks. We may think of the spots as being bradded or stapled together at

the appropriate holes. Thus, for example, $J_2^{27}(R^4,1^3)$ would be drawn in
the second system of graphical syntax as in Figure 10.

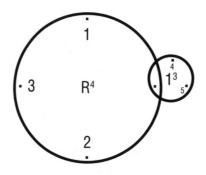

Before discussing Join$_1$ in the second system of graphical syntax, we need
to discuss the construction of identity relations.

It was noted in Theorem 7.1 that the identity relation ID^2 may be constructed from teridentity in the manner indicated by the graphs in Figure
11, which are drawn using the first graphical system.

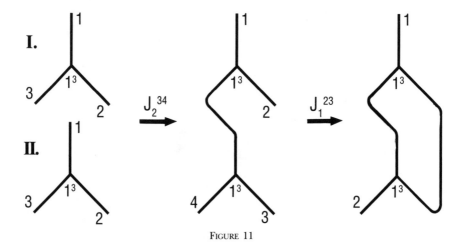

Similarly, the construction of ID^4 may be represented as in Figure 12.

At this point, it should be easy to see how, in terms of the first system of
graphical syntax, any identity relation ID^n, for $n > 3$, may be represented as
constructed from teridentity alone.

Now in the second system of graphical syntax, the construction of the
dyadic identity spot (Figure 13) from teridentity spots alone may be drawn

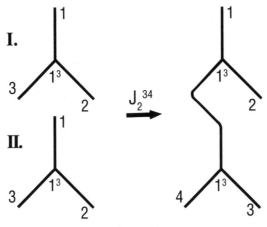

FIGURE 12

as in Figure 14. Similarly, the quadric identity spot could be drawn as in Figure 15, and it is easy to see how the method can be extended.

FIGURE 13

FIGURE 14

FIGURE 15

Let us now generalize. From Corollary 7.1.1, we know that, for all Enterpretations (D,*) of PAL and for all i, j such that $1 \leq i \leq n < j \leq n + m$, we have that

$$*[J_2{}^{ij}(1^n,1^m)] = *(1^{n + m - 2})$$.

So it is clear that a chain of two joined (by $Join_2$) spots of identity is semantically equivalent to some single spot of identity. By induction it follows that a chain or network of any number of joined (by Join$_2$) spots of identity is semantically equivalent to some single spot of identity. Thus, we may, in the second system of graphical syntax, link together identity spots to form what we might call *lines of identity*. Lines of identity are simply lines that are themselves composed of spots of identity of various adicities that are directly joined together (which represents their being joined together by Join$_2$). Thus, for example, the line of identity (Figure 16), when seen in magnification, might look something like Figure 17.

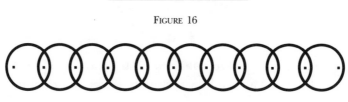

FIGURE 16

FIGURE 17

This line of identity would, of course, be equivalent to the dyadic identity spot. Similarly, the more complex line of identity (Figure 18),

FIGURE 18

when seen in magnification, might look something like Figure 19.

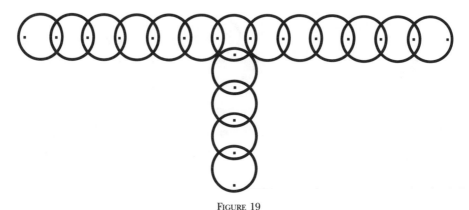

FIGURE 19

We may now discuss how the operation J_1^{ij} is drawn in the second system of graphical syntax. This operation is drawn by running a line of identity, which is constructed from purely dyadic identity spots, between the appropriate two hooks (holes). For example, in the second system of graphical syntax, $J_1^{23}(R^4)$ might be drawn in magnification as in Figure 20.

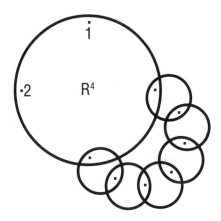

Figure 20

Permutations may be represented by renumbering in a straightforward way the lines or holes that represent hooks. Note that permutations apply only to elements of PAL. Now elements of PAL appear in graphical syntax always as 1-piece graphs. (The chorisis of a term corresponds to the number of separate connected pieces of a graph.) If a given permutation moves whatever is in the ith position to the jth position, it is depicted by renumbering the ith hook with the number j, for all the hooks.

Negation may be represented graphically by drawing a simple closed curve on the graphing surface in such a way that the curve encloses precisely those portions of the graph that are intended to be within the scope of the negation involved. Like permutation, negation applies only to elements of PAL, and thus negation is represented in graphical syntax by a simple closed curve that encloses some single connected piece of a graph. In the first system of graphical syntax, the radiating lines that represent hooks should be extended to the outside of the simple closed curve that depicts NEG. For example, in the first system of graphical syntax, $NEG(R^4)$ would be drawn as in Figure 21.

In light of the KPRODUCT operators, by which any array of PAL may be replaced by a single element of PAL, the limitation on the applicability of

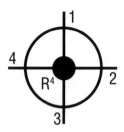

FIGURE 21

permutation and negation only to elements turns out to be of no special importance, except with regard to the theorems about compositeness and degeneracy.

The COMMA operator is represented in graphical syntax by attaching a spot of teridentity to the spot upon which COMMA is understood to operate by connecting any one of the hooks of teridentity to the hook numbered by the superscript of the COMMA operator. Thus, for example, $COMMA^3(R^5)$ would be represented in the first graphical system by the graph in Figure 22.

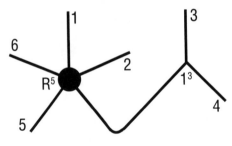

FIGURE 22

In the second graphical system $COMMA^3(R^5)$ would be drawn as in Figure 23. Note that in both systems, the free hooks are renumbered in an obvious manner. The QUANT operator is represented in graphical syntax by attaching a spot of teridentity that already has two of its hooks connected together to the hook numbered by the superscript of the QUANT operator. Thus, for example, $QUANT^3(R^5)$ would be represented in the first graphical system by the graph in Figure 24.

In the second graphical system $QUANT^3(R^5)$ would be drawn as in Figure 25. Unmagnified, this would appear as in Figure 26, where it is understood that the line of identity is attached to the third hook of R^5. Note again that in both graphical systems, the free hooks are renumbered in an obvious fashion.

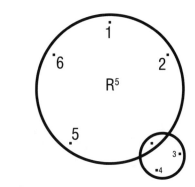

FIGURE 23

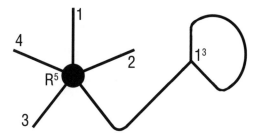

FIGURE 24

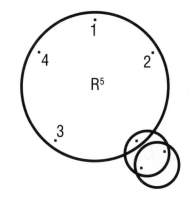

FIGURE 25

FIGURE 26

The representation of the ADID operators and the HOOKID operators in the first system of graphical syntax may be seen from the following examples. ADID^{135}(R^5) is depicted by Figure 27. HOOKID^{135}(R^5) is depicted in the first graphical system by Figure 28.

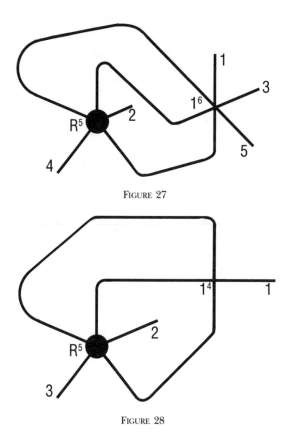

FIGURE 27

FIGURE 28

The renumbering of free hooks is accomplished in an obvious fashion.

Representing the ADID and HOOKID operators in the second system of graphical syntax is very much like representing them in the first system. Thus, ADID^{135}(R^5) is depicted (partially magnified) by Figure 29. HOOKID^{135}(R^5) is depicted (partially magnified) by Figure 30. Again, renumbering of free hooks is done in an obvious fashion.

By using the examples given, readers should now be able to draw in graphical syntax any of the constructions appearing in the algebraic presentation of PAL. Readers should also be able to use the examples to help understand more readily the algebraic constructions themselves.

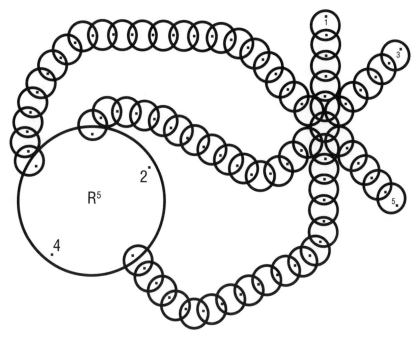

FIGURE 29

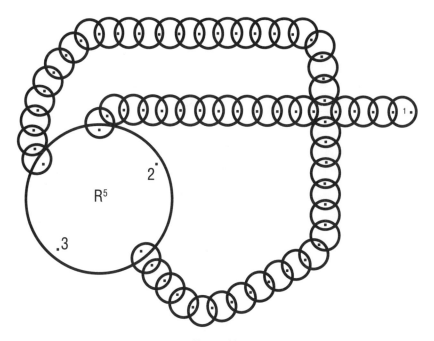

FIGURE 30

1. See, for example, Hartshorne, *et al.*, 1958, 4.347-4.584, for discussions by Peirce on graphical logic.

CONCLUDING REMARKS
ON THE CONSISTENCY AND COMPLETENESS
OF PEIRCEAN ALGEBRAIC LOGIC
AND ITS POTENTIAL VALUE

In this work, owing to its limited scope and focus, the topic of the deductive apparatus for PAL has been omitted. It can, indeed, be shown that PAL may be fitted out with a deductive apparatus with respect to which PAL is both consistent and complete. Indeed, PAL may be fitted out with a consistent, complete deductive apparatus that is similar to the system of illative permissions of Peirce's existential graphs. A full discussion of this matter, however, would approximately double the length of this work, which is already overly lengthy. Accordingly, this discussion must be reserved for another work.[1]

PAL's potential value lies in two, and perhaps even three, directions. First, there is, of course, its potential value for clarifying the logic of Peirce, especially in connection with Peirce's existential graphs. Secondly, PAL has the potential to lead to novel results both in mathematical logic on the one hand and in graph theory on the other. PAL may also turn out to have relevance for some branches of topology. For in connecting, as it does, two domains of investigation that heretofore have been isolated from one another, PAL has the potential to enable the derivation of results in the one domain by means of achieving results in the other domain. Historically, when two previously separate domains of investigation have been connected—as, for example, in Descartes's connecting of algebra and geometry—the outcome has been the achievement of significant new understandings in both domains.

If Peirce scholars conclude that the formalism of this work represents with reasonable faithfulness Peirce's own thinking about his réduction thesis, then this work should also have broad relevance for interpreting Peirce's semeiotic and his theory of categories. Indeed, it should serve to help vindicate a great many claims that Peirce put forth. Even if this work should be thought by Peirce scholars to diverge substantially in certain respects from Peirce's thinking, it should at least serve to hint at Peirce's genius as a mathematical logician. It should also indicate the futility of attempting to refute Peirce's thinking merely by adducing examples of well-known historical reductions to the dyadic; more generally, it should indicate the idleness of attacking Peirce by the mere means of a facile juggling of logical symbols.

Naturally, many questions will be raised by this work. Some of them will be somewhat technical in character. For example, the work raises the question as to exactly what Peirce thought about the permutation operations. In the early sections of this work, the permutations were presented as *basic* operations of PAL. The reason for presenting them as thus basic was because Peirce often seems to consider them as fundamental. Yet the permutations could very well be *omitted* from the basic operations of PAL, because they are in fact derivable from $Join_2$ and 1^2. In order to see this, consider again the permutation

$$\begin{bmatrix} 1, 2, 3, \ldots, i-1, i, i+1, \ldots, n \\ 1, 2, 3, \ldots, i-1, n, i, i+1, \ldots, n-1 \end{bmatrix} \quad,$$

which was called CYCLE(n,i) in Section 7. And recall that this permutation moves whatever is in the ith position to the last (n^{th}) position while shifting what is in positions i+1 through n one place to the left. Now, in terms of this (sort of) cycle, we may define *every* permutation P_i^n, where P_i^n is the *inverse* of the permutation

$$\begin{bmatrix} 1, & 2, & \ldots, & n \\ p(1), & p(2), & \ldots, & p(n) \end{bmatrix} \quad,$$

so that P_i^n moves whatever is in position $p(1)$ to position 1, whatever is in position $p(2)$ to position 2, and so forth. For, CYCLE(n,i) has the effect of simply moving the ith entry to the *last* (n^{th}) position; so, if we first move whatever is in position $p(1)$ to the last position, then move whatever is in position $p(2)$ to the last position, and then continue on until we have moved whatever in in position $p(n)$ to the last position, we will have moved whatever is in position $p(1)$ to the first position, whatever is in position $p(2)$ to the second position, and so forth. Thus, the permutation P results. The procedure can be defined more exactly as follows.

For each j, with $1 \le j \le n$, let n_j be the number of integers in the list $p(1)$, $p(2), \ldots, p(j-1), p(j)$ that are *strictly less* in magnitude than $p(j)$; and let $i_j = p(j) - n_j$. Then it is straightforwardly verifiable that the permutation P_i^n is given by the product (composition) of cycles:

$$CYCLE(n,i_n)CYCLE(n,i_{n-1}) \ldots CYCLE(n,i_2)CYCLE(n,i_1) \quad.$$

Now, because this is the case, it suffices for showing that the permutations may be derived from $Join_2$ and 1^2 to show that CYCLE(n,i) may be defined in terms of $Join_2$ and 1^2. We may here ignore adicity 0, because the permutations apply only trivially in this case. So, for $n \ge 1$, let E^n be any element of PAL, and let $(D,*)$ be any Enterpretation. Let $*(E^n) = X^n$, where X^n is the class (matrix) of n-tuples over D:

$$\{(\delta_1, \delta_2, \ldots, \delta_n)\} \quad .$$

And let i be such that $1 \leq i \leq n$. *Then*:

$$*[J_2^{i,n+1}(E^n, 1^2)]$$

$$= DEL^{i,n+1}\{SEL^{i,n+1}[*(E^n) \times *(1^2)]\}$$

$$= DEL^{i,n+1}\{(\delta_1, \ldots, \delta_{i-1}, \delta_i, \delta_{i+1}, \ldots, \delta_n, \delta_i, \delta_i)\}$$

$$= \{(\delta_1, \ldots, \delta_{i-1}, \delta_{i+1}, \ldots, \delta_n, \delta_i)\}$$

$$= *[CYCLE(n,i)(E^n)] \quad .$$

Because the permutation operations may thus be presented as derived operations of PAL rather than as basic ones, the problem is to account for Peirce's thinking about permutation operations and for any historical changes his thinking may have undergone.

Other questions this work raises will be more broadly philosophical in character than the question as to Peirce's thinking about the permutations. For example, in connection with Peirce's theory of categories, the question will be raised as to why the Junction operations should be considered as somehow more "fundamental" than, let us say, the Boolean Product; and in connection with Peirce's theory of identity, the question will arise as to why identity should be considered to be "basically" or "essentially" triadic rather than dyadic. Philosophical questions of this sort will be, of course, predictably difficult to settle. Nevertheless, they must be pursued. Accordingly, this work will have served its purpose well enough if only it stimulates a reader here or there to accept my invitation to pursue these questions.

NOTES

1. Hints that a basically Peircean system of deduction for PAL does indeed exist can be found throughout Peirce's writings on existential graphs. The author of the present work intends to publish an account of such a system in a future volume.

BIBLIOGRAPHY

Bernays, Paul
    1959   Über eine natürliche Erweiterung des Relationenkalküls, in *Constructivity in Mathematics*, ed. Arendt Heyting. Amsterdam: North-Holland.

Biggs, N. L., Lloyd, E. K., and Wilson, R. J., eds.
    1976   *Graph Theory 1736-1936*. Oxford: Oxford University Press.

Brunning, Jacqueline
    1981   Peirce's Development of the Algebra of Relations. Dissertation, University of Toronto.

Chang, C. C. and Keisler, H. J.
    1973   *Model Theory*, Amsterdam: North-Holland.

Eisele, Carolyn
    1979   *Studies in the Scientific and Mathematical Philosophy of Charles S. Peirce*, ed. R. M. Martin. The Hague: Mouton.

Eisele, Carolyn, ed.
    1976   *The New Elements of Mathematics by Charles S. Peirce*. The Hague: Mouton.
    1985   *Historical Perspectives on Peirce's Logic of Science*. Amsterdam: Mouton.

Faris, J. A.
    1981   C. S. Peirce's Existential Graphs. *Bulletin of the Institute of Mathematics and its Applications*, 17: 226-233.

Gardner, Martin
    1958   *Logic Machines and Diagrams*. New York: McGraw-Hill.

Halmos, Paul
    1962   *Algebraic Logic*. New York: Chelsea.

Hartshorne, C., Weiss, P., and Burks, A., eds.
    1958   *Collected Papers of Charles Sanders Peirce*. Cambridge, Mass.: Harvard University Press.

Hawkins, Benjamin S.
    1981   Peirce's and Frege's Systems of Notation, in *Proceedings of the C. S. Peirce Bicentennial International Congress*, ed. K. L. Ketner, J. M. Ransdell, C. Eisele, M. H. Fisch, and C. S. Hardwick. Lubbock: Texas Tech University Press.

Henkin, Leon
    1955   The representation theorem for cylindrical algebras, in *Mathematical Interpretation of Formal Systems*. Amsterdam: North-Holland.

Herzberger, Hans G.
    1981   Peirce's Remarkable Theorem, in *Pragmatism and Purpose: Essays Presented to Thomas A. Goudge*, ed. L. W. Sumner, J. G. Slater, and F. Wilson. Toronto: University of Toronto Press.

Ketner, Kenneth Laine
    1981   The Best Example of Semiosis and its Use in Teaching Semiotics. *American Journal of Semiotics*, 1: 47-84.
    1982a Carolyn Eisele's Place in Peirce Studies. *Historia Mathematica*, 9: 326-332.
    1982b Peirce's Existential Graphs as the Basis for an Introduction to Logic: Semiosis in the Logic Classroom, in *Semiotics 1980*, comp. M. Herzfeld and M. D. Lenhart. New York: Plenum.
    1984   Peirce on Diagrammatic Thought, in *Zeichen und Realität*, ed. Klaus Oehler. Tübingen: Stauffenburg Verlag.
    1985   How Hintikka Misunderstood Peirce's Account of Theorematic Reasoning. *Transactions of the Charles S. Peirce Society*, 21: 407- 418.
    1986a Semiotic is an Observational Science, in *Iconicity: Essays on the Nature of Culture*, ed. P. Bouissac, M. Herzfeld, and R. Posner. Tübingen: Stauffenburg Verlag.
    1986b Peirce's "Most Lucid and Interesting Paper": An Introduction to Cenopythagoreanism. *International Philosophical Quarterly*, 25: 375-392.

1986c *A Comprehensive Bibliography of the Published Works of Charles Sanders Peirce, with a Bibliography of Secondary Studies,* second ed., revised. Bowling Green: Philosophy Documentation Center.

1989 "Hartshorne and Peirce's Categories," in *Hartshorne, Process Philosophy, and Theology,* ed. R. Kane and S. H. Phillips. Albany: State University of New York Press.

Ketner, Kenneth Laine, ed.

1983 A Brief Intellectual Autobiography by Charles Sanders Peirce. *American Journal of Semiotics,* 2: 61-84.

Kloesel, C. J. W., Fisch, M. H., Ziegler, L. A., Roberts, D. D., Houser, N., Houser, A., Niklas, U., and Moore, E. C., eds.

1982 *Writings of Charles S. Peirce: A Chronological Edition, Vol. 1, 1857-1866.* Bloomington: Indiana University Press.

1984 *Writings of Charles S. Peirce: A Chronological Edition, Vol. 2, 1867-1871.* Bloomington: Indiana University Press.

1986 *Writings of Charles S. Peirce: A Chronological Edition, Vol. 3, 1872-1878.* Bloomington: Indiana University Press.

Kripke, Saul A.

1959 A Completeness Theorem in Modal Logic. *Journal of Symbolic Logic,* 24: 1-15.

Kuratowski, Kasimierz

1930 Sur le problème des courbes gauches en topologie. *Fundamenta Mathematicae,* 15: 271-283.

Listing, Johann Benedict

1847 Vorstudien zur Topologie. *Göttinger Studien,* 1,II: 811-875.

1862 der Census räumlicher Complexe, oder Verallgemeinerung des Euler'schen Satzes von den Polyëdern. *Abhandlungen der Königlichen Gesellschaft der Wissenschaften zu Göttingen,* 10: 97- 182 mit Tafeln.

Löwenheim, Leopold

1915 Über Möglichkeiten im Relativkalkül. *Mathematische Annalen,* 76: 447-470.

Lyndon, R. C.

1950 The Representation of Relational Algebras. *Annals of Mathematics,* 51: 707-729.

Mendelson, Elliott

1987 *Introduction to Mathematical Logic.* Belmont, Ca.: Wadsworth & Brooks/Cole.

Menzel, Christopher

1986 A Complete, Type-free "Second-order" Logic and Its Philosophical Foundations. Technical Report No. CSLI-86-40. Stanford: Center for the Study of Language and Information.

Murphey, Murray G.

1961 *The Development of Peirce's Philosophy.* Cambridge, Mass.: Harvard University Press.

Palmer, W. G.

1944 *Valency, Classical and Modern.* Cambridge: Cambridge University Press.

1965 *A History of the Concept of Valency to 1930.* Cambridge: Cambridge University Press.

Putnam, Hilary

1982 Peirce the Logician. *Historia Mathematica,* 9: 290-301.

Quine, W. V. O.

1966a Reduction to a Dyadic Predicate, in *Selected Logic Papers.* New York: Random House.

1966b Variables Explained Away, in *Selected Logic Papers.* New York: Random House.

1971 Predicate-Functor Logic, in *Proceedings of the Second Scandanavian Logic Symposium,* ed. J. E. Fenstad. Amsterdam: North-Holland.

1972 Algebraic Logic and Predicate Functors, in *Logic and Art: Essays in Honor of Nelson Goodman,* ed. R. Rudner and I. Scheffer. New York: Bobbs-Merrill.

Roberts, Don D.

1973 *The Existential Graphs of Charles S. Peirce.* The Hague: Mouton.

Schröder, Ernst
    1966   *Vorlesungen über die Algebra der Logik (exacte Logik)*. New York: Chelsea.
Skidmore, Arthur W.
    1971   Peirce and Triads. *Transactions of the Charles S. Peirce Society,* 7: 3-23.
Tarski, Alfred
    1941   On the Calculus of Relations. *Journal of Symbolic Logic,* 6: 73-89.
    1952   A Representation Theorem for Cylindrical Algebras. *Bulletin of the American Mathematical Society,* 58: 65-66.
Thibaud, Pierre
    1975   *La Logique de Charles Sanders Peirce: De l'algebre aux graphes*. Aix-en-Provence: Université de Provence.
van Heijenoort, Jean, ed.
    1966   *Source Book in Mathematical Logic, 1879-1931*. Cambridge, Mass.: Harvard University Press.
White, Arthur T.
    1973   *Graphs, Groups, and Surfaces*. Amsterdam: North-Holland.
Whitney, Hassler
    1932   Non-separable and Planar Graphs. *Transactions of the American Mathematical Society,* 34: 339-362.
Zeman, J. Jay
    1964   The Graphical Logic of C. S. Peirce. Dissertation, University of Chicago.

INDEX

Abstraction, hypostatic. *See* Hypostatic abstraction

Adicity, vii, 3, 8
  consistency with, of elementary derivations of PAL, 12-13
  of assemblies of PAL, 20
  of classes of n-tuples, 29
  of element-candidates of PAL, 12
  of finite sequences of relations-simpliciter, 40
  of primitive terms of PAL, 12-13
  of relations-simpliciter, 40
  of sequences of classes of n-tuples, 30
  of terms of PAL, 12-16, 18-19

Adicity places. *See* Hooks

ADID operator, 81-85
  generalized, 83-85
  graphical syntax for, 134-135

Application of relations to relations, x, 2-4

Arraying, x

Arrays of PAL, 13, 16-19
  adicity of, 18
  canonical, to represent assemblies of PAL, 21-22
  census Theorem for, and for assemblies of PAL, 21
  chorisis of, 18
  cyclosis of, 18-19
  definition of, 16-17
  edge count of, 18
  in assemblies of pal, 20-21
  of length 1, 17, 24, 44
  retracting, 17-19
  size of, 18
  valency rule theorem for, and for assemblies of PAL, 21
  vertex count of, 18
  writing, 17

Assemblies of PAL, 19-21
  adicity of, 20
  as potentially expressing and representing relations, 24
  census theorem for arrays and, 21
  chorisis of, 20
  cyclosis of, 20
  edge count of, 20
  size of, 20
  valency rule theorem for arrays and, 21
  vertex count of, 20
  writing, 20

Augmentation by hypostatic abstraction. *See* Hypostatic abstraction

Bag, 20

Bernays, Paul, x, 1, 5, 17, 20, 34, 35, 81, 120

Betti numbers. *See* Listing numbers

Block of matrix of n-tuples, 29-30, 33

Bonding, logical and chemical, 3-4

Bonding algebra, vii, x

Boolean algebra, 1

Boolean sum, 120

Boolean product, 92, 120, 139

BOOLEPRODUCT operator, 92

Cartesian factor, 32

Cartesian product, 31-32, 41-42
  and compositeness, 46-51
  and concatenation, 7-8
  and degeneracy, 47-51
  role of, in depiction, expression, and representation, 47-51

Categories, theory of, 117, 137, 139

Census theorem
  of J. B. Listing, 3, 5, 8, 13
  for arrays and assemblies of PAL, 21
  for elements of PAL, 15-16

Chemistry and logic, 3-4

Chorisis, 8, 53, 54
   of assemblies of PAL, 20-21
   of terms of PAL, 12-16, 18-19
Church, Alonzo. *See* Church's thesis
Church's thesis, 122
Classes of n-tuples, 27-30
   compared to sets, 28
   identity, 30
   notation for, 30
   universal, 5, 30
   zero, 30
Classes of 0-tuples, 28-29, 30. *See also* Truth values
Coincidence, 98
Column of a matrix of n-tuples, 29, 76-78
Column-vector notation, 29
COMMA operator, viii, 76-92
   as applied to elements of adicity 0, 79-80
   as doubling a column of a matrix of n-tuples, 76-78
   effect of, as reversed by HOOKID operator, 83
   graphical syntax for, 132-133
Complementation, 31, 41
Completeness of PAL, 137
Compositeness of relations-simpliciter, 46-51
Concatenation, 97. *See also* Cartesian product
Conjunction, generalized, 88-92
Consistency of PAL, 137
Consistency with adicity of elementary derivations, 12-13
Constructibility
   and degeneracy of relations, 53-65
   of a relation, 55-56
   of a term of PAL, 54
Construction
   Peircean operations of. *See* Derivation, Peircean operations of
   of assemblies, 54

of relations from relations, x, 53-65, 71-92
   Of terms of PAL, 19, 53-65
Corner quotes, use of, 7
Correspondence of an Enterpretation of PAL with an interpretation of QL, 98, 102
CYCLE operators, 77-78, 82, 138-139
   as used in defining COMMA operator, 77-78
   as definable from Join_2 and 1^2, 138-139
Cyclosis, 8
   of assemblies of PAL, 20-21
   of terms of PAL, 12-16, 18-19
Deductive apparatus for PAL, 137, 139n
Degeneracy, 47-51, 53-65
   of reducible dyadic relations, 59-60
   of reducible triadic relations, 60-64
   of relations reducible to monadic and/or dyadic relations, 63-64
Deletion operations
   general, 35, 42
   singly-indexed, 35
DeMorgan, Augustus, 2
Denotation of relations-simpliciter
   by constant primitive terms of PAL, 21
   by arrays of PAL, 48-49
Depiction
   of sequences of classes of n-tuples by arrays of PAL, 37-38
   of sequences of relations by arrays of PAL, 22, 48-49
Derivation, Peircean operations of, x, 53-54
Derivative, immediate, of an assembly, 53-54
Derivative of an assembly, 54
Derived elements of PAL, 75-92
Derived operations of PAL, 76-92
Descartes, René, 137
Disjunction, 92
Domain of enterpretation, 28
Domains of sufficiently large cardinality, vii, xi n4, 110-113

Double-deletion operations, 34-35

Dyadic relations

all, as constructible from triadic relations alone, 78

constructibility of all zero-adic relations from, 75

Irreducibility of non-degenerate, 59-60

Issue of reducibility to, vii, viii, 57-58, 60-64, 117-122

reducibility of degenerate, 59-60

Edge count

of assemblies of PAL, 20-21

of terms of PAL, 12-16, 18-19

Element-candidates of PAL, 12-13

Elementary derivations, 12-13, 15-16

Elementary terms of PAL. *See* Elements of PAL

Elements of PAL, 10-16

adicity of, 13-14

census theorem for, 15-16

chorisis of, 13-14

cyclosis of, 13-14

definition of, 12-13

derived. *See* Derived elements of PAL

edge count of, 13-14

of adicity 0, 13, 79-80

primitive terms of PAL as, 13

size of, 13-14

valency rule theorem for, 14-15

vertex count of, 13-14

Enterpretation, 27-38

compared with interpretation, 27

domain of, 28

of Pal, defined, 36

of PAL corresponding to an interpretation of QL, 98, 102

Enterpretation function, 27, 36, 38

Equivalence, logical, of terms of PAL, 38

Entitative graphs, 2

Entities, 106, 113

Euler, Leonhard, 2, 3, 8

Euler-Poincaré formula, 3, 8. *See also* Census theorem

Existential graphs, vii, viii, ix, x, 2, 3, 5, 123-135, 137

Expressibility of relations by terms of PAL, 48-51

Expression

direct, of relations by primitive terms of PAL, 22

extensional, of classes of n-tuples by arrays of PAL, 37-38

intensional, of relations by arrays of PAL, 48-49

of relations by terms of PAL, 21-24

potential, by assemblies of PAL, 22

Extensional semantics for PAL. *See* Semantics for PAL

Extensional valuation function. *See* Enterpretation function

Extensionalism, viii-x

FALSE, the 0-adic relation, 40, 74

First-order logic with identity. *See* QL

Formulae, well-formed, of PAL. *See* Well-formed formulae

Foundationalism, metaphysical, with respect to relations, ix

Four-color map problem, 2

Frege, Gottlob, 3, 6n4, 10

Function

defined, 28

determined by an interpretation of QL, 96-97

Extensional valuation. *See* Enterpretation function

Intensional valuation. *See* Intensional valuation function

Functor calculus, Quine's, 1

Genus. *See* Torus

Gödel-von Neumann-Bernays set theory. *See* Set theory, Gödel-von Neumann-Bernays

Graph theory, vii, viii, 8, 137

Graphical syntax for PAL, 7, 10, 123-136

Halmos, Paul, 1

Harvard University, 3

Henkin, Leon, 1

Herzberger, Hans G., vii, viii, ix, x, 1, 110, 112, 113, 114

Herzberger theorem, intensional, 114-115

Herzberger's theorem, 110-112

HOOKID operator, 81-87

    as usable to reverse the effect of COMMA operator, 83

    commutivity of, with NEG operator, 86-87

    generalized, 83-85

    graphical syntax for, 134-135

Hooks, 10

    as doubled up by COMMA operator, 76-78

    free, 126

    junction operations as joining two, 23

    lines as picturing, in graphical syntax, 124

    holes as picturing, in graphical syntax, 124

Hypostatic abstraction, viii, ix, 105-116

    and higher-order logic, 121

    augmentation of an enterpretation by, 108-109

    augmentation of an interpretation by, 113

    various forms of, 115-116

Iconicity, 2-3

Identifying variables. See ADID; HOOKID; Variables

Identity

    as dyadic in standard logical literature, 71

    as irreducibly triadic in PAL, 71-72, 139. See also Teridentity

    lines of. See Lines of identity

Identity class of n-tuples, 30

Identity relations, 9-10, 40, 129-130

    all, as constructible from teridentity alone, 72-73

    graphical syntax for. See Lines of identity; Teridentity

    non-degeneracy of, 70

    non-degeneracy of complements of, 70

Illative permissions, 137

Intensional semantics for PAL. See Semantics for PAL

Intensional valuation function, 43-44

Intensionalism, viii-x

Interpretation, 27, 39

    compared with enterpretation, 27

    of PAL, defined, 43-44

Interpretation function, ix. See also Interpretation

Interpretation of QL. See QL, interpretation of

Ions, 3-4

Irreducibility

    of non-degenerate dyadic relations, 59-60

    of non-degenerate triadic relations, 60-63

    of odd-adic relations to even-adic relations, 58

    of odd-adic terms to even-adic terms, 57-58

    of zero-adic and 1-adic relations, 57

    Of zero-adic and 1-adic terms, 56-57

Iteration, 54

Johns Hopkins University, 2

$Join_1$ operator, 11-12, 36, 45, 125-131, 139

$Join_2$ operator, 11-12, 36, 45, 125-128, 139

Joining, 3, 10. See also $Join_1$; $Join_2$

Junction operations. See also $Join_1$; $Join_2$; Joining

Junction operations, fundamental nature of, 139

Kant, Immanuel, 3

Kempe, Alfred Bray, 2, 120

Ketner, Kenneth Laine, vii, viii, ix, 121

KPRODUCT operators, 90-92

Kripke, Saul, 27, 39

Kripke structures, 27

Kuratowski, Kazimierz, 2

Lexicographical ordering, 29, 30

Lines of identity, 128-130

Listing, Johann Benedict, 2, 3, 6n2, 8, 13

Listing numbers, 8

Logic
   algebraic, vii, viii, x, 1, 2, 5, 10
   contemporary, viii
   modal. *See* Modal logic
   of Peirce, vii, viii, ix, 1, 3, 5, 137
   quantificational, 1, 8, 9, 22, 27, 75, 76,
      81, 91, 92, 93, 106. *See also* QL
         standard, nominalistic, ix
Loose ends. *See* Hooks
Löwenheim, Leopold, vii, xin2, 118, 120
Lyndon, R. C., 1
Marks of reference, 1, 6n1
Matrix of n-tuples, 29-30, 33
Matrix of wff of QL in prenex normal
   form, 93-103
Menzel, Christopher, 122n
Mind, ix
Mitchell, O. H., 1
Modal logic, 27
   Peirce's, ix
   possible world semantics for, 39
Model structures, 40, 51n, 70
Monadic relations
   all, as constructible from triadic relations
      alone, 75
   irreducibility to, of non-degenerate
      dyadic relations, 59-60
   irreducibility of, 57
   reducibility to, of degenerate dyadic
      relations, 59-60
NEG operator, 10
   and negation, 91
   commutativity of, with HOOKID
      operator, 86-87
   semantics for. *See* Complementation
Negation, x, 10
   and NEG operator, 91
   and PRODUCT operator, 88
   graphical syntax for, 131
   semantics for. *See* Complementation
Nominalism, ix
Non-composite relations, existence of, 67-70

Non-degeneracy of identity relations and
   their complements, 70
Non-degenerate relations, existence of,
   67-70
N-sequences, 28
N-tuples, 28-29. *See also* Classes of
   n-tuples; Matrix of n-tuples
Null n-tuples, 28-29
Null relations, 40
   all, as constructible from teridentity
      alone, 74-75
   degeneracy of, 51
Nullity, 8. *See also* Cyclosis
Obtainings of a relation, 106-108, 113
Operations, Peircean, of construction
   (derivation), 10-12. *See also*
      Derivation, Peircean operations of;
      Iteration; Join$_1$; Join$_2$; Negation;
      Permutation
PAL. *See* Peircean algebraic logic
Palmer, W. G., 3
Pegs, xv. *See also* Hooks
Peirce, Benjamin, 3
Peirce, Charles Sanders
   algebra of dyadic relations of, xv
   argument of, for reduction thesis, vii
   compared with Frege, 3, 6n4, 10
   existential Graphs of. *See* Existential
      graphs
   foundationalism of, with respect to
      relations, ix
   historical influence of, xi n2
   intensionalism of, viii-ix
   logical project of, 1-6
   modal logic of, ix
   realism of, with respect to relations, ix
   reduction thesis of, vii-viii
   semeiotic of. *See* Semeiotic
   theory of categories of. *See* Categories,
      theory of
   understanding of relations of, viii-ix
   unitary logical vision of, 3-6

view of, regarding fundamentality of
    junction operations, 139
view of, regarding nature of permutation
    operations, 138-139
Peircean algebraic logic
    semantics of, extensional, 27-38
    semantics of, intensional, 27, 28, 39-51
    syntax of, 8-25
Peirce'sche Produkt. *See* Application of
    relations to relations
Permutations, x, 10-11, 41
    as derived operations of PAL, 138-139
    CYCLE operators as species of, 77-78
    graphical syntax for, 131
    inverse of, 31
    major, x
    minor, x
    view of Peirce regarding nature of, 138-139
Permutation operators, 31, 41, 77
Pieces, separate connected, of a graph,
    8. *See also* Chorisis
Poincaré, Henri, 3, 8
Possible world, 39, 40
Primitive terms of PAL, 8-10
    adicity of, 12-13
    as correlated with predicate symbols of
        QL, 93
    as directly expressing relations, 22
    as elements, 13
    augmentation with respect to. *See*
        Hypostatic abstraction
    chorisis of, 13-14
    constant, 9-10, 22
    cyclosis of, 13-14
    edge count of, 13-14
    size of, 13
    vertex count of, 13-14
PRODUCT operator, 87-92
PROPROD operator, 88-90
Properties of terms of PAL, 12-16, 18-19.
    See also Adicity; Chorisis; Cyclosis;
    Edge count; Size; Vertex count

QL, 93-104
    closed sentences of, 97
    function determined by an
        interpretation of, 96-97
    interpretation of, 96-103
    interpretation of, corresponding to an
        enterpretation of PAL, 98, 102
    primitive terms of PAL as correlated with
        predicate symbols of, 93
    satisfaction in an interpretation of, 96-97
    translation in PAL of a wff of, 93-96, 102-103
    truth in an interpretation of, 96-98
QUANT operator, 81, 132-133
Quantification
    empty, 93, 103
    in QL, translation into PAL of, 95-96
    redundant, 93, 103
    treatment of, in PAL. *See* QUANT
        operator
Quantification theory, 1, 2. *See also* QL
Quantifier, concept of, 1
Quine, Willard Van Orman, vii, x, xi n5,
    1, 118, 120-121
Realism of Peirce with respect to
    relations, ix
Reducibility
    and degeneracy, 57, 59-64. *See also*
        Degeneracy
    of a relation, 55-56
    of a term of PAL, 54-55
Reducible relations, existence of, 57
Reducible terms, existence of, 57
Reduction. *See* Construction
Reduction theorem for PAL
    consistency of, with results of
        Löwenheim and Quine, vii, 117-122
    extensional, 109-110
    intensional, 113-114
Reduction thesis, vii-x, 3, 4, 5
    negative part of, 4, 117, 120
    negative results concerning, 59-64, 67-70
    positive part of, 75

positive results concerning. *See* Reduction theorem for PAL

"Relation," as used for "relation-simpliciter," 48

Relations, vii-x, 3
  as understood in the sense of sets of n-tuples, viii
  as such. *See* Relations-simpliciter
  dyadic. *See* Dyadic relations
  in intension. *See* Relations-simpliciter
  logic of, ix
  monadic. *See* Monadic relations
  triadic. *See* Triadic relations relations-simpliciter, viii-ix, x, 2, 27, 39-51
  adicity of, 40
  degeneracy of universal and null, 51
  identity. *See* Identity relations
  null. *See* Null relations
  universal. *See* Universal relations
  zero-adic, 40

Relative product. *See* Application of relations to relations

Representation of relations by terms of PAL, 21-24

Representation
  extensional, of classes of n-tuples by arrays of PAL, 37-38
  intensional, of relations by arrays of PAL, 48-49

Representation theorem for PAL, 102-103

Retracting
  arrays of PAL, 17-18
  sequences of classes of n-tuples, 30-33
  sequences of relations-simpliciter, 41-42
  role of, in depiction, expression, and representation, 48-51

Retraction. *See* Retracting

Russell, Bertrand, xv

Satisfaction, 39, 96-97

Schröder, Ernst, vii, xi n2

Selection operations, general, 34-35, 41, 42

Selective double deletion operations, 11-12, 31, 33-35, 41, 42

Self part of a dyadic relation, 35

Semantics
  logical, ix
  modal, 27, 39

Semantics for PAL
  extensional, 27-38
  intensional, 27, 28, 39-51
  symbols for, 42-43

Semeiosis, 93

Semeiotic, ix, 1, 137

Sequences of classes of n-tuples, 30-33

Sequences of length 1, 7, 30, 32, 40, 42

Sequences of relations-simpliciter, 40-42

Set that indexes all domains, 39

Sets, compared to classes, 28

Set theory
  Gödel-von Neumann-Bernays, 27
  Zermelo-Fraenkel, 27, 28

Size
  and compositeness, 48-51
  and degeneracy, 49-51
  of assemblies of PAL, 20-21
  of terms of PAL, 12-16, 18-19

Skidmore, Arthur W., 107

Spots, xv, 123-125
  of identity, 125, 127, 128-129. *See also* Lines of identity
  of teridentity, 125

Streichung, 33, 34, 35, 81, 120

Subsuming, of a relation by a relation, 25

Sylvester, J. J., 2

Symmetric group, 10

Syntax, topological, 2

Tarski, Alfred, 1, 96

Teridentity, viii, 9, 71-92, 117
  constructibility of all identity relations from, 72-73, 128-130
  constructibility of TRUE and FALSE from, 74
  graphical syntax for, 125. *See also* Lines of identity

Terminology, Peirce's compared with contemporary, 8

Terms of PAL, 8-25. *See also* Arrays of PAL; Elementary terms of PAL; Primitive terms of PAL; Properties of terms of PAL

Thesis that all constructional procedures are formalizable in PAL, 121-122

Thirdness, 117-122

Topological syntax for logic, 2-3

Topologie, the word. *See* Topology

Topology, 2, 3, 5, 137

Torus, 2, 125

Translation. *See* QL, translation in PAL of a wff of

Triadic relations

  constructibility of all dyadic relations from, 78

  constructibility of all monadic relations from, 75

  constructibility of all zero-adic relations from, 78-79

  irreducibility of non-degenerate, 60-63

  reducibility of degenerate, 60-63

Triple-Junction, 120

TRUE, the 0-adic relation, 40, 74

Truth

  for primitive wffs of PAL, 38, 44

  for wffs of QL, 96-98

Truth values, 28, 31

Tunnel bridge, 125

Tuples, 29

Turing, Alan, 122

Universal relations, 9-10, 40

  all, as constructible from teridentity alone, 73-74

  degeneracy of, 51

Unsaturated positions. *See* Hooks

Use-mention distinction, 7

ULV. *See* Peirce, Charles Sanders, unitary logical vision of

Valency, 3

Valency analysis, vii

Valency equations, 4

Valency formula, 3-4

Valental positions, 3. *See also* Hooks

Valental number, 3. *See also* Adicity

Valency rule theorem

  for arrays and assemblies of PAL, 21

  for elements of PAL, 14-15

Van Heijenoort, Jean, 120

Variable-occurrences of QL

  and hooks, 98-103

  in well-formed formulae of QL, 93-103

Variables

  in well-formed formulae of QL, 93-103

  identifying free, 93-96, 120. *See also* ADID operator; HOOKID operator

  marks of reference as rudimentary. *See* Marks of reference

Vertex count

  of assemblies of PAL, 20-21

  of terms of PAL, 12-16, 18-19

Victoria Lady Welby, xv

Well-formed formulae

  of PAL, 24-25

  of QL, 93-104

Whitehead, Alfred North, xv

Whitney, Hassler, 2

Zermelo-Fraenkel set theory. *See* Set theory, Zermelo-Fraenkel

ZFC. *See* Set theory, Zermelo-Fraenkel

Zero-adic elements. *See* Elements of PAL, of adicity 0

Zero-adic relations, 40

  all, as constructible from dyadic relations alone, 75

  all, as constructible from triadic relations alone, 78-79

  irreducibility of, 57

  TRUE and FALSE, as constructible from teridentity alone, 74

Zusammenfügung, x, 5, 17